FEMINAZIS

Psycho-social portrait of extreme feminism and the risks of politically correct thinking dictatorship

Felix Daniel Wilson - Tamara López.

Betty Friedan once told Simone de Beauvoir that women should have the option of staying at home to raise children. Beauvoir replied that they shouldn't have her, since, if not, too many would choose her.

It is time to say that a certain derivation of the feminist movement has resulted in a group that is very authoritarian - with respect to the life that other women must have - very violent and that, above all, everyone is afraid to talk and dislike them.

Everyone is afraid of being accused of *"male chauvinist pig"*.

The mythological idea of "Patriarchy" is complemented by the dangerous idea of "Femicide".

Femicide is a murderer who kills on behalf of the Patriarchy.

Some homicides are considered "Femicides".

This violence is implemented from the new Gender Courts or Gender Justice, where the burden of proof is reversed, since each defendant is guilty not as a singular human person, is guilty as a member of the oppressive and murderous collective. Therefore, self-defensive violence, based on sentences that deprive the home, visits to children - and even freedom - to men - as members of the oppressive group - is implemented based on this type of "Justice".

This Hegelian justice -which judges collective- that replaces liberal individualist justice -which judges individuals-, and that reverses the burden of proof - they expel you from your home, they imprison you, all without evidence, with the single complaint- it calls a lot attention to jurists, but no one dares to speak for fear of being accused of "patriarchal."

Therefore, the slogan "KILL YOUR BOYFRIEND, YOUR FATHER AND YOUR CHILD" can be seen painted on the walls, murderous violence that is self-defensive against the members of the oppressive collective, who are previously dehumanized.

It is true that homicide rates are higher in men, but it is also true that homicide victims are 90% male and, moreover, that, in recent years, feminazi propaganda has been increasing the number of women who they kill their partners, which are held openly in feminazi demonstrations.

They are a very violent and dangerous movement, but no one dares to criticize him for fear of receiving the accusation of "macho", which makes up the dictatorship of politically correct thinking.

The Feminazis have been so successful in imposing their slogans that no one dares to criticize them anymore and "the politically correct thing" is to ingratiate themselves with them, conceal their actions, and allow them to present themselves as the eternal victims of an evil entity that digits everything and for the which everyone should answer: *"The Patriarchy"*

Many times the organizers of the demonstrations separate themselves from the "excesses" of some "violent deviants". But, in truth, they do very little to criticize the alleged deviants, because they know that they would lose the leadership of the feminist movement which has become radicalized and - inevitably - violent.

On the other hand, they have some internal problems that are most striking, as is the case with the space of the prostitutes - or sex workers - within the movement.

Often, some women who practice prostitution - and who have their own agenda of discrimination, inhuman treatment, rape or abuse by the police, among other claims - want to demonstrate and participate in these movements. The problem is that for the feminist central discourse, prostitution is a consequence of "Patriarchy", and then the other feminists are deeply disturbed by the very existence of women who, not happy to work in prostitution, do not accept to adapt their presentation same to the script of the exploitation of the "Patriarchy"

The Feminazis, then, join the more conservative right to claim, for example, that women dress more and ban fashion shows and pornography. However, its list of prohibitions is more demanding than those of the conservative right.

One of the tactical objectives of the organizations they have - which move hundreds of millions of dollars - is to destroying the contents of the educational programs. The main idea is to graft the "gender perspective" that, according to the authors, needs to change the two fundamental institutions of the Patriarchy: marriage and family.

Indeed, in recent years, the so-called "feminist movement" has gained attention, which, in its most radicalized facet, gives rise to this new urban tribe: the Feminazis.

It is important to say that these feminists, in turn, arrogate the leadership role of all women in this imaginary battle of the sexes but that, of course, a large part of women do not feel in any way represented by feminists.

It happens that they have an undeniable authoritarian and paternalistic vocation. Feminazis refer to women who do not agree with their manifestations as *"dominated by patriarchy"* and that is why they self-attribute the tutelage of the latter in a superior way.

We are going to study the emergence of this phenomenon, feminazis, what they want, their ideological bases and, above all, the social psychology of their success, or of their arrival in increasingly large groups of the population.

It is a mass phenomenon that follows the logic of violent pressure groups and the political psychology of the friend-enemy, but is integrated by ideological elements and historical roots that are necessary to understand and that will be the object, in this book, of a thorough exploration.

Feminazis are highly combative, violent and intolerant and, for these reasons, have an important capacity to generate fear and, consequently, influence. Indeed, they have an important firepower capable of destroying the prestige of any person who makes a political career, or even journalists. This leads to a cautious attitude with them from the "opinion makers" and, consequently, that install your slogans, still devoid of scientific evidence to support them, as a hegemonic discourse.

The wedge is closing against those who dare to raise their voices and put some light on the contradictions of their claims, because they are quickly cataloged as "right" or "macho" and that stains them with a stigma of discrimination that closes them doors. In this way, the social identities of the influential people need to ingratiate themselves with the "feminazis" as an obliged party not to receive such heavy artillery attacks and thus keep their place.

For that reason, the unique thought is becoming more and more demanding and as well as a group, although initially small (rarely supported by the bulk of the women), receives a powerful influence in the democracy that ends up consecrating situations that, although if they are unfair, they are popularly seen as a kind of general "revenge" of a sector that presents itself as oppressed.

Thus, for example, we not only find politicians (more and more) who strive to have the support (demanding support) of the noisy feminazis and journalists (who try to reduce the coverage of their excesses - destroyed cities, painted churches, slogans murderers- and to expand the visibility of what shows them well), but there are also judges. This book will also present the philosophical and legal bases of the new feminazis courts, as well as the reason that supports them, the so-called "gender violence".

The fundamental feminazi slogans are:

a) The "inclusive language".

b) "Gender awareness."

c) Legal discrimination according to gender, through "gender quota" or others to reverse the "glass ceiling".

d) Legal abortion, financed by the state and "safe".

e) The existence of the "Patriarchy" and the "patriarchal culture".

f) Femicide, a concept that consists of attributing to the "Patriarchy" the authorship of some homicides, as well as the "gender violence" that is based on the endorsement of the Patriarchy of the authorship of certain forms of domestic violence.

Indeed, the slogans of the feminists, which will be subject to careful and thorough exploration in this book, lack technical, scientific and academic support, but, for the reasons of sociology of power already described - specifically, all strive to look good with them, because doing so serves on the ladder to power politicians, journalists and judges - and nobody dares to discuss them. You can't even get into the rational debate, partly because the foundations of the movement are deeply irrational - we will discuss the psychology of the Feminazi - but, above all, because the rhetorical artillery of the Feminazi resorts to the ad hominem fallacy (to personal disqualification) to destroy their critics, and thus be able to exemplify and that nobody else dares to exercise them.

This book, then, is first and foremost a book of sociology and social psychology, because debating "rationally" something that has irrational bases would be a) too easy (for reason, they give up the feminine slogans) b) too useless (because the attempt it would not help to understand the reasons for the phenomenon). Then it is better to know the irrational deep foundations that account for the phenomenon and, together with its historical origins, will be approached with depth and documentation.

We can only anticipate, in this introduction, that the term "Feminazi" is very descriptive for these purposes, because it serves to underline its aspiration for unique thinking, its violence, its resentment and various specific characteristics that underlie the genesis and strength of the movement, to its bases, which will be the object of careful development in this book, with scientific support. It is correct to call them "Feminazis" and this will be neatly developed in the chapter dealing with feminazi social psychology.

Is it really bad to use the Nazis as a form of criticism of ideologies that are radical, violent and authoritarian and that foster stereotypes and dehumanization? We disagree It can be, instead, a way of having the living memory of the tragedy and an invitation to rationality, respect, diverse opinions and distrust groups of enlightened people who believe the owners of truth.

There is a claim that is typical of these groups: the claim to impose the way we should talk.

Therefore, we have the right to express ourselves with this same concept, to understand it, to develop it, to propose new views from the serenity of the argument. To carry out a study a) on feminazis as a radicalized group b) on the social characteristics that allow its appearance, its development and its apogee.

II- FEMINISM AND FEMINAZIS. TWO DIFFERENT THINGS.

It is important to recognize, from these pages, the feminist movement that, in its historical moment that justified it, achieved social changes that allowed the world to be a fairer place.

In this regard, we should mentioning a fallacy - or dishonest rhetorical trick - that feminazi groups can use frequently: the straw man.

A straw man is a form of argument and an informal fallacy based on giving the impression of refuting an opponent's argument, while actually refuting an argument that was not presented by that opponent.

One who engages in this fallacy is said to be "attacking a straw man".

The typical straw man argument creates the illusion of having completely refuted or defeated an opponent's proposition through the covert replacement of it with a different proposition (i.e., "stand up a straw man") and the subsequent refutation of that false argument ("knock down a straw man") instead of the opponent's proposition.

Straw man arguments have been used throughout history in polemical debate, particularly regarding highly charged emotional subjects.

In this case, the straw man is to accuse those who speak of feminine groups of being insulting "the entire feminist movement." So to anyone who dares to question the legitimacy of any claim, the feminazi artillery quickly attributes it to trying to criticize the entire feminist movement.

One of the great discomforts brought by a public debate where the straw man fallacy abounds, is that the point of view itself must be clarified again and again, to try to shield it against malicious misrepresentations. However, it is useless to do so, because the foundations of feminazis are - as will be carefully studied - irrational and irrational positions can never be rationally criticized.

In spite of that, - and although we can anticipate that the misrepresentation will be inevitable - it is worth clarifying that they are two different things:

a) feminism

b) radicalized and extremist feminism.

The important break is when feminism stops claiming Equality and begins to claim Inequality because of a victim's position -

victim's position that is intrinsic to extremist and violent ideas--

Feminism involves the idea of equal treatment in all aspects of life between all sexes and refusing to be subordinate to those who demean them due to their sex.

Feminism was the gateway for women to achieve the right to vote.

Feminists encourage women to hold themselves with self-respect.

It is undeniable that changes in important areas such as the right to education, the vote of women, the right to work, equality before the law, were partly achieved or promoted by historical feminists.

Being a woman is a characteristic with many others.

Being a woman does not define a person's identity or their ideas. Each woman is much more than her mere biological sex, and can claim not to be pigeonholed by her mere characteristic. Each person is much more than a mere characteristic.

A person can be a woman, shy, ambitious, intelligent, short stature, coming from high social extracts, brown hair, blue eyes, Christian religion, simple dress, classical musical tastes ... etc. etc (among hundreds of many possible features).

When any of these characteristics is relevant to the law, we start talking about discrimination. One can speak, for example, of historical times in which other people, by the mere fact of having the characteristic of having black skin, could not always enjoy freedom. On those occasions, when a particular characteristic causes "inequality before the law" towards those who have it, then any movement that struggles to re-establish the affected human dignity is legitimate.

Today, for example, unborn people have fewer rights than born people. Even in some countries the state facilitates the murder of unborn people. Then, there is an inequality and the movements that try to recognize the person for the birth of the same rights - above all, the right to life - that people who have already been born are legitimate.

Feminism was a movement that initially also fought for equality, equal rights between men and women.

It developed in England, the United States and other parts of the world throughout the eighteenth century until the early twentieth century. He concentrated on obtaining equality against men in terms of property rights and equal capacity to act, as well as the demand for equal rights within marriage. Feminism then demanded the incorporation of women into the academic world. It took force in the 18th century with bourgeois revolutions, claiming legal equality and access to citizenship for women

Many feminist authors and activists, mostly from the United States and the United Kingdom, take feminism to the field of activism, especially in a context of vindication of equal rights. In addition, historical events of the moment, especially the abolition of slavery, will be very influential in the future of the feminist movement, being able to find a correlation between the struggle for abolition and the struggle for women's rights: many of the leaders of this first current they are wives of abolitionist leaders.

This was how the characteristic of being of a race motivated legal discrimination as well as that of being of a certain gender, so both groups - often related - claimed equality before the law.

Therefore, we make it clear that Feminism - as a historical movement that fought for the equal rights of women - is not the recipient of the criticisms of this book or that here it is not called feminazis to those people who, quite the opposite of a Nazi, demanded greater equality before the law.

Although any person who uses the word "feminazi" will be maliciously misrepresented and accused of criticizing the entire feminist movement - and not its radicalized version - it is important to clarify anyway that feminists are not equal to feminazis.

Feminazis, on the other hand, have different ideological bases and different claims.

Feminism is part of the egalitarian movements - which sought equality for people who, by some characteristic, were legally discriminated against and had fewer rights -, together with the abolitionism of slavery, the abolitionism of religious or racial persecutions, the struggles against xenophobias and active militancy against other prejudiced ideas.

Instead, feminazis are part of the conspiracy historical movements that seek to blame an Other - be it another of religious beliefs, another of race, another of nationality, another of thought, another of sexual gender - of all public misfortunes

Therefore, we make it clear that Feminism - as a historical movement that fought for the equal rights of women – deserve respect and recognition. Although anyone who uses the word "feminazi" will be maliciously misrepresented and accused of criticizing the entire feminist movement - and not its radicalized version - it is important to clarify anyway that feminazis are not equal to feminists.

-III- IDEOLOGICAL CONTENTS OF THE FEMINAZIS. THE PATRIARCHY AS A FUNDAMENTAL CONCEPT OF FEMINAZISM.

Feminazis are people who have a violent and intolerant action that is due to a) a group of ideological beliefs of lack of rational consistency b) a specific psychology that leads to rabid those beliefs.

The mistake of discussing "a" is that, what sustains the situation, is really "b" and, therefore, a debate based on arguments and reason cannot be reached.

However, although b) is left for further study in subsequent chapters, the ideological contents will be briefly described or reviewed.

The fundamental basis rests on what has been called "gender ideology" and also "gender consciousness." All this aimed at a dialectical enemy, "The Patriarchal Culture" or "The Patriarchy" or also "Heteropatriarchy."

The concept of "gender ideology" has been criticized, saying that it is a derogatory epithet about political positions, underlining that there are diverse gender perspectives, etc.

However, the "gender ideology" is the theoretical trunk on which its different slopes emerge and all of them are characterized by the dialectical struggle against an oppressive entity that could be called "The Patriarchy", the "Hetereopatriarchy", "The Patriarchal Culture".

What is Patriarchy?

Patriarchy literally means "the rule of the father".

Historically, the term Patriarchy has been used to refer to autocratic rule by the male head of a family.

Patriarchal societies, according to anthropology, are those in which there is a "Patriarchy." The Patriarchy is a legal and social order is bound to the figure of the Patriarch who is the Head of a large family, commonly an elder.

As head of a large family, the patriarch had to provide for many people, including servants. A typical household consisted of the patriarch, his wife, children, servants and slaves, and many other member of the family that were under his roof.

You can think of the Old Testament, where some Patriarchs were fathers of numerous descendants and, in turn, socially and legally legitimized as the highest authority, father and legal authority.

In today's society the highest political, legal and social authority is not the Patriarch and, within families, sometimes the authority is mixed, sometimes the father, sometimes the mother, sometimes an uncle is more important. It depends on the personality of each member of the couple, there is a lot of variation.

Precisely, because it is not a patriarchal society.

However, feminazis make their own conceptual construction of the "Patriarchy" that is a central part of their ideology.

It is an omnipresent concept but never clearly defined.

The Patriarchy is - in essence - a very powerful imaginary Entity that exercises the oppression of women.

It could be understood as a tacit agreement between men where the supremacy of the male and the oppression of the woman is imposed.

"The common erotic project of destroying women makes it possible for men to unite into a brotherhood; this project is the only firm and trustworthy groundwork for cooperation among males and all male bonding is based on it" wrote the feminist Andrea Dworking.

"The arbitrary character of patriarchal ascriptions of temperament and role has little

effect upon their power over us. Nor do the mutually exclusive, contradictory, and polar qualities of the categories "masculine" and "feminine" imposed upon human personality give rise to sufficiently serious question among us. Under their aegis each personality becomes little more, and often less than half, of its human potential. Politically, the fact that each group exhibits a circumscribed but complementary personality and range of activity is of secondary importance to the fact that each represents a status or power division. In the matter of conformity patriarchy is a governing ideology without peer; it is probably that no other system has ever exercised such a complete control over its subjects" Kate Millet.

This Imaginary Entity (*"The Patriarchy"*) could also be understood as an unconscious cultural force (the "patriarchal culture") that operates and influences the behavior of people to provoke the oppression of women

Then "patriarchal culture" surpasses the minds of all people and predisposes them to harm or oppress - or give a lower place - to women ... or also to murder them.

The society resulting from this "patriarchal culture" would be a society made up of "oppressors" (men) and "oppressed" (women).

Some currents also speak of the "Hetero-patriarchy". This imaginary entity is more effective to position as a victim not only women, but, fundamentally, sexual minorities who decide to have a non-hetero partner.

The concept of "Hetero-patriarchy", as a dialectical enemy, has succeeded in increasing the participation of sexual minorities within this victimization framework that underpins gender ideology - that is, let's look for an imaginary enemy not only for resentful women, but also for gays or resentful lesbians-, but, for greater expressive ease, we speak of "Patriarchy" (where the "Hetero-patriarchy" wants to subsume also).

Patriarchy is a "Reification".

Reification is the treatment of something abstract as a material or concrete thing. Reification occurs when relations between things are mistakenly taken to be either entities themselves or intrinsic properties or qualities of things

Reifying is characteristic of pseudosciences, where gender ideology rests and leads to explanations that seem easy. In this case, the Patriarchy, a concept that had initially been proposed to explain some characteristics of a social order - fundamentally, historical social orders, of nomadic peoples -, takes on a life of its own as a Frankestein who awakens and begins to act as a Devil who, with his own personality, digits the silent threads that lead to maintaining the oppression of women.

This type of rhetorical technique (giving a concept a life of its own) is common in postmodernist authors, but it is very bad from the point of view of scientific rigor.

"When observed events are attributed to some hidden inner entity, not only is scientific inquiry deflected toward the impossible task of understanding the hidden entity, but also curiosity tends to rest. Further inquiry is impeded not only by the seeming difficulty of the task, but also by the semblance of an explanation being taken for the real thing" William M Baum.

Someone looking for concrete things may ask:

Where is the Patriarchy?

Who are they?

Answers to these questions cannot be given, because it has given its own personality to what was originally a concept. First a concept is "reified" (It is given the value of a true and real thing), then it is "personalized" (it is given person attributes, decisions, it is described as if it were a villain king in the shadows).

Gerda Lerner, in her 1986 *The Creation of Patriarchy*, makes a series of arguments about the origins and reproduction of Patriarchy as a system of oppression of women, and concludes that Patriarchy is socially constructed and seen as natural and invisible.

Shulamith Firestone, defines Patriarchy as a system of oppression of women. Firestone believes that Patriarchy is caused by the biological inequalities between women and men, e.g. that women bear children, while men do not.

Firestone writes that patriarchal ideologies support the oppression of women and gives as an example the joy of giving birth, which she labels a patriarchal myth.

For Firestone, women must gain control over reproduction in order to be free from oppression.

Th Patriarchy, in short, is a very powerful abstract entity that seeks to harm women and maintain their oppression.

You can read sentences like these:

"Since ancient times, heteropatriarchy has shaped the way how societies across the world have viewed masculinity and femininity"

"Heteropatriarchy creates an environment of oppression and inequality for racial and sexual minority groups. Heteropatriarchy depends upon the perspective of gender roles, in which men are considered strong, able, and

intelligent and females are depicted as weak, unable, and naive. The gender and sex identities created and protected by the projected status quo ensures the power of heterosexual man in a regime of compulsory heteropatriarch"

"To manage this issue, capitalism uses patriarchy as a lever to attain its objectives, while at the same time reinforcing it.

The fact that women are relegated – by patriarchy – to domestic tasks allows capitalists to justify their over-exploitation and under-payment of women with the argument that their work is less productive than men's. "

These texts become very difficult, precisely because they are full of reifications, concepts that are given the quality of "things" and that take on a life of their own.

Feminazi ideology is influenced by constructivist and, above all, postmodernist philosophical currents.

Foucault, or Gilles Deleuze, can be considered influential.

Foucault, for anyone who has scientific interests - science points to concrete, material, objective realities - is a disaster, but enjoys a lot of prestige and influence in the humanities faculties of some countries.

Constructivists, likewise, raise a questioning of the "objectivity" of any discourse, which leads to the frustration of anyone who demands that they speak clearly about concrete things.

Postmodern authors write in a very heavy, intentionally dark language.

The logic of Andersen's story *"The Emperor's New Clothes"* is given. Is a short tale about two weavers who promise an emperor a new suit of clothes that they say is invisible to those who are unfit for their positions, stupid, or incompetent – while in reality, they make no clothes at all, making everyone believe the clothes are invisible to them.

When the emperor parades before his subjects in his new "clothes", no one dares to say that they do not see any suit of clothes on him for fear that they will be seen as stupid. Finally a child cries out, *"But he isn't wearing anything at all!"*

In the same way, everyone pretends to understand something clear when talking about the imaginary entity *"The Patriarchy"* that justifies the dialectical battle, although in these speeches you can never see something clear.

In fact, at the metaphysical level postmodernism is Anti-Realistic. This means that *"There is no independent reality"* to describe, that is replaced by the discourse that is had, which makes the viewer's gaze.

With respect to the "Patriarchy", then, it does not exist as something concrete, although it is inferred from the texts that it would be an imaginary powerful Entity that pursues female oppression.

To begin to approach, briefly, the postmodernists we must first go to Hegel - who with "his son" Marx - is the great antecedent of the feminazi ideology.

Hegel criticizes Kant, notes that Kant is trapped in Aristotelian logic, that another type of reason is needed. He distances himself from the illustration and begins to "speak weird." Although Hegel is intentionally obscure , it raises some bases that will be important later in the postmodernists and in the concept of Patriarchy that sustains all the feminazi discourse.

Reason, for Hegel, is a more collective than individual function.

Individuals are built by the cultures that surround them, which, in turn, are a function of deep forces. The individual is an emerging aspect of a larger whole, the collective. In addition, conflict and contradiction are the deepest truths of reality.

There is no reason, but feelings and, above all, contradictions between entities that lead a dialectical battle.

This current gives impunity to have contradictory and inconsistent ideas. If the contradiction is pointed out to them, postmodernists can respond *"they are nothing more than positivist contradictions, of scientific logic, of Aristotelian logic"*, they are on a higher level of thinking where everything is relative, everything can be raised and the only certain thing It is the conflict of groups

As philosopher Stephen Hicks explain: *"Postmodernism is the first ruthlessly consistent statement of the consequences of rejecting reason, those consequences being necessary given the history of epistemology since Kant."*

The postmodernist view is that truth doesn't exist or discovered in any objective sense, but truth is linked in a circular relation to the systems of power which promote it, and to the effects of power which truth itself generates.

According to the Postmodernism, all of us are conditioned by our society and language, and no one is actually free to engage a universe with objectively true statements of fact. Postmodernism celebrates diversity and contingent or situated meaning and rejects universal solutions. Anything goes and nothing is certain.

Reified constructions - or academic metaphors about phenomena that are then taken as real entities - are common in this type of currents that make the feminazi ideology.

According to Foucault and his followers the modern 'episteme' is constituted by three planes: the a priori sciences (e.g. maths); the a posteriori sciences (e.g. biology); and philosophical reflection. The Foucauldians argue that the human sciences do not exist on any of these three planes.

"It's my hypothesis that the individual is not a pre-given entity which is seized on by the exercise of power. The individual, with his identity and characteristics, is the product of a relation of power exercised over bodies, multiplicities, movements, desires, forces" Foucault.

Accordingly, there is freedom to invent abstract imaginary entities, without offering evidence that they exist.

For example, Foucault, in his book "Disciplinary Power", refers to a "Power" that is responsible for supplying the capitalist market of disciplined workers.

But who is that "Power" that wants to subdue us? Where is him?

In "History of Madness," Foucault tells us about a "Normalizing Power" typical of the Psychiatric Hospital, which, with the help of certain knowledge, would normalize normality.

Foucault says that Power is, above all, a positive technology that produces things: architectures, institutions, speeches, knowledge, truth, scientific statements, laws, habits, regulations, identity, subjectivity, ways of socializing, individuals, ways of thinking, of being and of living.

The Power, then, is a reified abstract entity that operates, from a beyond, the behavior of all individuals - both those who exercise that Power, and their victims - and no one seems to realize that it is managed by that Power.

The only way to escape from this "Power" that wants to direct our lives and "build us" is the singularity, although the latter is not very well defined either.

For example, Judith Butler takes the idea of oppressive power and discipline. She argues that "gender" is a discipline by the patriarchal power, with Foucault influence.

For Butler, the concept of "The Woman" has been disciplined from the medical, psychological, etc. discourse. Therefore, it is intended to unmask this intentional construction and deconstruct, to make visible behind this construction, -always behind the veil, is the secret -... the various mechanisms of patriarchal power.

The debates between "biologists-constructivists" focus on the question of whether culture builds us - especially builds our gender and hence our behavior - or if there is a certain genetic basis, but something central is out of focus to understand these perspectives: paranoid.

The current of thought on which feminazis is based is based on abstract Entities that oppress us, that prevent us from being free, that "discipline" us, that force us to have a certain life oriented to the ends of those Entities. Authors pretend free ourselves by "opening our eyes" to those who move our threads, class interests or gender.

For example, Gilles Deleuze says *"Now, there is no doubt that trees are planted in our heads: the tree of life, the tree of know of knowledge, etc.   The whole word demands roots. Power is always arborescent. "*

These abstractions ("The Power", "The Disciplinary Society" and, a conceptual child of all this, The Patriarchy) take on a life of their own and strive to direct our lives according to their evil ends, but everything is so secret that - Unless we "get free" with these readings - we never know that we are oppressed and managed.

From his side, it is very clear that Foucault inspired one of the founding authors of the so-called Radical Feminism: Kate Millet.

Thanks to Millett's influence, feminist criticism assumes that social life is "symbolic" and materially divided into two genders. In addition, these genres are "built."

And who built them? The power. Who is the power? The Patriarchy

Therefore, the idea is to attack this deception that "has been imposed on us" and, from there, question the political and economic stratification, the sexual division of labor, the distribution of roles and, ultimately, all social categories. All of them can secretly be a "construction" of the oppressive designs of the Patriarchy.

From authors such as Millet, Firestone, Friedan, the gender ideology, influenced by Foucault, takes its conspiracy theory. There are, then, two realities: "the one who told us" (the patriarchal secret power) and "the one that underlies the secret" (the reality of the oppression of the Patriarchy). Therefore, these authors present their intellectual exercise as an act that leads to "Unmasking" a reality that is hidden, the reality of oppression conspired by the power in the shadows, The Patriarchy.

"If knowledge is power, power is also knowledge, and a large factor in their subordinate position is the fairly systematic ignorance patriarchy imposes upon women." Kate Millett, Sexual Politics

"Your only mistake then was in trusting the people who brought you here." I will hear this remark for the rest of my life: it will echo along the walls of my mind until all sound stops for me." Kate Millett, The Loony-Bin Trip

There is also an influence of Hegel and Karl Marx.

For Hegel we are not individual people, but built and part of groups that are in conflict. For Marx, we are divided into "social classes," the Marxist superstructure comes to mask the reality of class conflict, but only if we take "class consciousness" can we recognize this underlying truth. Those workers who do not feel solidarity for their class, who do not act in defense of their class, who do not act - in short - as representatives of their collective, it is because they lack "class consciousness" or - worse - because the social class antagonist - the bourgeoisie - has inoculated the ideas of the superstructure, so that they can never see the secret conflict that underlies.

Within radical feminism, this reality of the two groups that collide is not that of the social classes, but of the genders. Therefore, radical feminist authors suggest that they will run the veil and show the action of the oppressive Power, The Patriarchy, it is a Power - as a reified entity, or as a devil entity as a villain king -

"I urge you to sin. But not against these itty-bitty religions, Christianity, Judaism, Islam, Hinduism, Buddhism-or their secular derivatives, Marxism, Maoism, Freudianism and Jungianism-which are all derivatives of the big religion of Patriarchy. Sin against the infrastructure itself" Mary Daly

"Personal is political," radical feminists would say. The things we do and that we believe are natural and our decisions; indeed, they are secretly influenced by the Patriarchy that pressures men to play the role of oppressors and women the role of oppressed.

The woman would always be in struggle against the army of cultural forces of the Patriarchy that oppresses her.

Betty Friedan, in her famous work *"The Feminine Mystique"* implies these super-powerful conspiracy forces that push women to have children, to have children is to give up the Patriarchy.

Friedan says:

"When a culture has erected barrier after barrier against women as separate selves; when a culture has erected legal, political, social, economic and educational barriers to women's own acceptance of maturity—even after most of those barriers are down it is still easier for a woman to seek the sanctuary of the home. It is easier to live through her husband and children than to make a road of her own in the world... It is frightening to grow up finally and be free of passive dependence. Why should a woman bother to be anything more than a wife and mother if all the forces of her culture tell her she doesn't have to, will be better off not to, grow up?"

Ok.

How do these forces speak ? Do they speak low or high? How do they whisper to women *"you don't have to grow up, you don't have to grow up"*?

Asking these questions is like telling the Emperor that he is naked. In postmodernist rhetoric the reification of concepts is common currency, that leads to abstraction going anywhere, so that the strangest conspiracy fantasies have a place.

"The key to the trap is, of course, education. The feminine mystique has made higher education for women seem suspect, unnecessary and even dangerous. But I think that education, and only education, has saved, and can continue to save, American women from the greater dangers of the feminine mystique." Betty Friedan.

The text is a good example of the two most common mechanisms of this discourse: a) reification and personification (Apparently an evil entity called "feminine mysticism" has attributes of person, because it does things, has made education look "suspicious") b) there is a "trap", therefore a "prelude", something hidden, the author unmasks the trap and shows us the actions of this evil entity that seeks to direct the lives of women.

This of speaking in metaphors - and then giving them life as if they had concrete social actions - can be exasperating for someone who wants clarifications, concrete things, but the appeal of the text is to inoculate a conspiracy idea.

In addition, it cannot be claimed that they say logical, real, scientific things, because, debtors of Hegel, they have an anti-rational theoretical position.

Therefore, the criticism of rationality and which begins with Hegel, is present in the ideological foundations of Feminazis, as well as collectivism. They are philosophical bases that encourage a perspective of permanent conflict between groups and from a cult towards irrationality, under a statement of paranoid roots.

"The Patriarchy" is then similar to the "Power" that Foucault speaks of, it is a supra-social, supra-legal, supra-personal entity, because it is beyond the people (oppressors and oppressed) who are only puppets.

The "Liberation" would be to escape from this Patriarchal Power or Oppressing Power, but, if you ask "Where is the Patriarchy?" "Who are they?" There is no answer 1) every feminazi is excused from giving rational answers thanks to Hegel 2) because, in reality, it is a "reification" - It is spoken in metaphors, every feminazi is exempt from giving details about what they want to say since, from relativism, there is no "reality to describe", but the discourse itself is what matters.

Faced with the complaint that the conspiracy they see has no empirical basis or logical basis or scientific basis, they may answer that it does not matter. What matters is the "anti-patriarchal" discourse that resists the oppression of the patriarchal discourse.

Therefore, in gender ideology there is a) a classification of people into collective representatives by their genitals b) a victimization of a collective that is presented as oppressed c) a .conspiracy theory based on a powerful, antagonistic entity, Maleficent and imaginary, "The Patriarchy" digits the threads to enable macho oppression.

In addition, this discourse is skeptical of the possibilities of the human being to direct his own destiny. So, to protect the masses, Art must be censored, because Art is often a tool of patriarchal culture. The vast majority of women would live deceived, without knowing that they are being managed by the inoculation of the patriarchal culture, the only way would be to change the culture for a "culture with a gender perspective".

Therefore, not infrequently they try to censor books, songs, movies and also artistic works.

The feminist Andrea Dworking says:

"We want to destroy sexism, that is, polar role definitions of male and female, man and woman. We want to destroy patriarchal power at its source, the family; in its most hideous form, the nation-state. We want to destroy the structure of culture as we know it, its art, its churches, its laws: all of the images, institutions, and structural mental sets which define women as hot wet fuck tubes, hot slits".

From this perspective, Art - then - in some cases, contributes to patriarchal oppression and must be destroyed, because it is Art that - as an arm of the Patriarchy - incites men to oppress women. Therefore, Art must be destroyed and replaced by a new, purer Art, more in line with the correct ideological precepts.

No matter how delusional all this authoritarianism is, it continues to be instrumented, because today it is the "politically correct" thing.

In general almost everything bad that can happen to a person - from not getting a job that he would like or not be reciprocated in love - if that person has the characteristic of being "woman", she can use the wild card to blame the "Patriarchy" of his own frustration.

Oppression of women, generated by patriarchal culture, would happen all the time. The oppressors would be men. All this reality would appear invisible to most people, but those who have "gender awareness" could recognize it.

The leaders, bearers of this well-known conscience, attribute leadership of a struggle of the entire feminine gender against what they call the "patriarchy" or, more abstractly, the "patriarchal culture." Therefore, it is a messianic leadership, or an enlightened elite, since the involuntary represented (all women) cannot kick or complain or ignore the leaders.

The appeal to "conscience" within the gender ideology, serves to throw an accusation to all women who do not support them to be in "non-conscience", so they are being denied any ability to think for themselves

"Every woman who has come to consciousness can recall an almost endless series of oppressive, violating, insulting, assaulting acts against her Self. Every woman is battered by such assaults - is on a psychic level, a battered woman" Mary Daly

Romantic Love would be an instrument of the Patriarchal Culture to perpetuate and chronicle the submission and submission of women. For radical feminists, for gender ideology, Romantic Love does not exist as a feeling, but is part of scripted and patriarchal stereotypes that impose the worst part on women and the best on men. That is why women who love a man are seen as dominated by the patriarchal culture and men who love a woman are understood as abusers.

Feminazis criticizes compliments, since, for feminazis, compliments are a form of violence. Many women report that they like to receive praise, that colleagues in the office tell them that they are beautiful or that they are well dressed or that they are intelligent. However, for feminazis this will be because they have no "gender awareness" and cannot visualize the implicit submission that represents listening to a compliment.

In addition, among other social and political changes that feminazis claim, are the famous "quotas" that determine to force a number of men or women in political positions, in representation in congresses, among other things. In reality, Patriarchy operates so that women earn less than men, so that there is a "glass ceiling" that prevents them from having good jobs.

The employer when hiring a person agrees to pay more to a "for being male" than what he would pay another "if it is a woman" for performing exactly the same function: Why, if the goal of the entrepreneur is to earn money and reduce costs and increase profitability?

Answer: to secretly fulfill the designs stipulated by the stereotypes of the patriarchal culture. In order to sustain the Patriarchy the businessman loses money from his own pocket, but this is "unconscious", because he is dominated by this patriarchal culture and he does not even know the threads that move it since it lacks a "gender perspective".

Therefore, the feminazi struggle would lead to the imposition of certain discriminations by law that increase a person's probability of coming to office for the sole reason of being a woman.

In addition, it is considered that the oppression of women by the Patriarchy is what underlies certain artistic and social manifestations and, therefore, constantly seeks censorship. In fact, the totalitarian vocation of radical feminism has led to the burning of books in demonstrations (books of "macho authors") and to make petitions to censor writers and poets.

In summary:

The ideology of the feminists is the so-called ideology of "gender" that postulates, in essence, that an oppression by men towards women would be perpetrated, the oppression would be naturalized by the "patriarchal culture". In turn, all this would be invisible to those who lack the awakening that the "gender perspective" means. On the other hand, the Patriarchy, a dialectical entity that justifies the struggle, would have a certain personality and operate silent threads of culture, art, media, to maintain oppression. As a result of this unequal, permanent and oppressive struggle, the feminazis, in an epic way, would be the heroines.

-IV- **THE LIE OF THE GLASS ROOF**

According to denounces the concept of the glass ceiling, men earn on average, more than women, and this is because the Patriarchy operates. In addition, it is the concern of some feminists that fewer women work in sectors such as engineering or systems.

However, in countries that have done more to reduce gender differences - like Scandinavian countries - people's decisions do not change. There is a proportion of 20 nurses female for every 1 nurse male, even in these countries. This can be explained in that women have more empathy than interests in certain more solitary jobs.

On the other hand, it is false that it is appropriate to divide people by a single characteristic and then check their result, as if that division were the only relevant thing.

Unlike what gender ideology intends, each person has a broad set of characteristics and each person is much more than each of those characteristics. The gender ideology takes away your individuality, your ability to be different, and makes you a representative of the collective, necessarily puts you in a collective and, therefore, only sees men and women as two divided and homogeneous groups-

What gender ideology does is make a cut in a characteristic (gender), highlight it in the light of observation, and then leave all other characteristics in the shade.

For example, introverts are less likely to be bosses. Then you could divide all people into "introverts" and "non-introverts" and then complain about quota of shyness and that all the shy can have a job of Chief, or that, at least, there is an equality of shy and not shy in leadership positions.

In fact, Scott and Kraimer (2001), made a study on the predictors of success of a professional career on a sample of 496 jobs from various organizations (318 men and 178 women). The best predictor of job success was not gender but proved to be this: "The extroversion."

Extroversion was related positively to salary level, promotions, and career satisfaction and that neuroticism was related negatively to career satisfaction

On the other hand, there was a strong negative predictor of success in customer care professions or that directly relate to the client in "kindness", those who had less of this personality trait had less chance of promoting in this type of companies.

Another of the data that is very well studied is that personal Beauty predicts success. In general, if a person has the characteristic of being pretty, it will be something more likely to be successful in his professional career. This is documented by numerous scientific studies, many of them grouped in *"Beauty Pays: Why Attractive People Are More Successful"* by Daniel S. Hamermesh

On the other hand, scientific studies that monitor statistics according to the various characteristics that a person can have have also shown a strong correlation between height and income. It is very well established that tall people have higher salaries, on average, than lower people (see, for example, the 2009 Hübler studies; Gao and colleagues 2010; Schultz, 2002, among many others).

In particular, a characteristic that predicts, according to statistics, very significantly that you will not be able to work from what you studied, is to have High-functioning Autism.

The Asperger or High-functioning Autism are forms of autism where the person can talk, can learn, can study, but ... generally does not get good jobs, or does not get any. People who have autism, even if they have adequate academic preparation, are much more likely to be unemployed or unable to work than they studied. Unemployment rates among Asperger sufferers are much higher than among the normal population (see, in this regard, the studies cited by Carley, 2016).

In general, autistic people who know how to speak the same have low-paid and medium-term jobs (see Hillier and Gallizi, 2014).

In fact, since 3 out of 4 people who have autism are male, the gender quota laws imposed by feminazis have effectively made it harder for us to see deputies or senators with autism.

Most people are not President of a company or manager or successful politician. And all these people can make a review of their personal characteristics (sexual gender, introversion or extroversion, emotional intelligence, if you have autism, if you have physical beauty, height, if you have humble origins or not, if you have facility for study, etc. etc. etc.) and you will find some of them that, according to statistics, will make it more unlikely that you will have a leadership position. Of course, for feminazis if there is another personal characteristic other than gender that makes it difficult for you to prosper or that makes it difficult for you, then it will be YOUR PROBLEM.

However, talking about the "Crystal Ceiling" is a lie, as a lie as saying that the only characteristic that predicts a person's destiny is whether he is male or female. Each person is a world, has many characteristics, some with advantages and disadvantages, in different aspects, different circumstances. And, above all, the scientific evidence is overwhelming in that there is no glass ceiling, but many glass ceilings ... so many that everyone can discover that they have their own glass ceiling.

-V- NAZIS AND FEMINAZIS. IDEOLOGICAL AND PHILOSOPHICAL BASES

It is important to emphasize that the underlying foundations, both in femininity and in Nazism, are not intellectual, but emotional. Therefore, the intellectual shell is very poor. It is not solid ideological or philosophical foundations that underpin ideology. There are other reasons that determine the success that, in some circumstances, these types of phenomena can have.

Hegel, the great critic of Aristotelian reason and defender of unreasonableness, within the worst of his legacy, proposed that people are not individual, but whether they want or not, representatives of groups that are in conflict, groups that collide. Therefore, these types of ideas use the voice "consciousness" a lot to discriminate against those who believe in them and those who do not, those who are not because they do not have "awareness" of their role as involuntary representatives of their own collective.

These precarious ideologies can choose a characteristic of people (sex, race, religion, skin color, social class, religious belief), generate two groups from dividing them by that characteristic and then propose a dialectic where one collective oppresses the other.

Karl Popper, in that great book that is "*The Open Society and its Enemies*" referred to the phenomenon as "tribalism." A personal characteristic is used to create a group membership and seeks a supremacy of the group over the other, instead of listening to all of us, instead of giving space to reason, to the debate of ideas.

"There is no doubt that the doctrine of the chosen people grew out of the tribal form of social life. Tribalism, i.e. the emphasis on the supreme importance of the tribe without which the individual is nothing at all, is an element which we shall find in many forms of historicist theories. Other forms which are no longer tribalist may still retain an element of collectivism: they may still emphasize the significance of some group or collective—for example, a class— without which the individual is nothing at all" Karl Popper.

Above all, the ideal precondition or breeding ground for these ideologies to grow is resentment at the frustration of individual goals. When a person, personally, feels very far from what he thinks he should be, then can choose to build his identity from belonging to a collective.

Laurie Rudman and Kimberly Fairchild (2007) show an experiment that was done to compare whether women's ugliness predicts their feminist inclinations.

More attractive female participants (using self-ratings) showed decreased feminist orientations, compared with less attractive counterparts.

On the other hand, from its side, Bordeau (2009) in his extensive study on xenophobia, shows that repeated research has shown a link between the increase in unemployment and the increase in xenophobia or political parties - from the extreme right - that express hatred abroad or racism.

With respect to the German tragedy of the Second War, the usual behavior is to treat them as "monsters" and dehumanize them.

This has two layers, the rest of humanity treats the Germans as monsters, the Germans treat the Nazis as monsters, but nobody wants to take care of what, as human beings, we can do to other human. From this perspective, however, it is lawful to assume these facts as potentially human (and not alien to us, not to blame outside), because it is the best way to prevent them from repeating themselves.

As Ron Rosenbaum says in his book "Explain Hitler: The search for the origins of his evil", Hitler was a person "like you or me" . *"Only a tremendously bleak version of human nature can find a Hitler, or even a potential Hitler, within each of us,"* insists Rosenbaum.

The harsh conditions of the Treaty of Versailles, precipitated not only the public humiliation of the pride of being German, but, above all, a great economic crisis that impacted by frustrating the individual life projects of hundreds of millions of people. The frustrated can no longer build their identity with their individual merits, so they are more likely to approach ideologies that allow them to be part of a group; Now you are no longer Mark, frustrated, unemployed, humiliated ... now you are "the working class" who is oppressed

For this reason, Marxism grew greatly in Germany after the Treaty of Versailles. Millions of frustrated workers could adopt the "class consciousness" proposed by Marx and blame the bourgeois social class for their own frustration. This, in turn, worried the German industrialists, who saw with fear this breakthrough of the "class struggle" dialectic.

Beyond that it is not the objective to summarize everything that happened here, it is important to say that, although there were many elements of the Nazi party that were openly leftist and socialist, like Goebbels, and although the red color of the flag had placed as a nod to the cause of the left, Hitler, influenced by Hegel - who did not see people, but groups in conflict - proposed to replace the "class struggle" with the "race struggle."

This proposal served to attract the frustrated middle class and German workers, but, in addition, to ward off the ghost of communism, so their cause soon gained support and financing from the industrialists.

From this perspective of the "race fight," Hitler built a unique enemy, an enemy that was to blame for all the frustrations of the frustrated and resentful people who approached his party. The enemy was an abstract entity, never very well defined, which was referred to as "The Jewry" or also "The international Jewry".

This entity was attributed an ominous power, in fact this entity typed all the threads of art, of the press, of culture, to secretly mobilize the Germans towards their failure. Although it is inconsistent from the rational, (but Hegel allows you incoherence), it was argued that both communism and capitalism were both secret designs of "The Jewry plan" to harm and drag the German people to defeat.

The representation of "The Jewry" as a super-powerful entity that typed all the threads of Germany towards its failure - using communism, the press, capitalism, art, everything - was possible when it was a small anti-system match However, if the imaginary reified entity as powerful as Nazism represented it, how did it allow it to rise to power? However, this response was given by blaming "The Jewry" for causing World War II.

In fact, Nazi propaganda, during the entire world war, as well as the contents that were modified from educational programs to graft this ideology to children, always represented the Germans - always, even within the top of the expansionist war - in the role of "The Victim" of global and evil conspiracy plots. Although the world later learned about the regime's atrocities, Hitler's followers, using the conspiracy card that nourishes this type of ideology, ignored history, ignored the evidence and continue to play the role of "The poor Victim" .

The collective delirium, once installed, leaves little room for free expression. Many important academics were expelled from universities for not expressing themselves in favor of the cause. In these cases, the climbers appear; if discrimination operated for many talented intellectuals to be expelled from universities and spaces, there was also an inverse discrimination because any mediocre, ambitious climber through the facility of "adapting to the right political thought" could rise in that society. Just as today many academics make a career thanks to adopting the "gender perspective", there were also climbers in Nazi Germany who adopted the "race perspective" .

The censorship of the Nazis towards the works of Art was manifested in "escraches" (a type of demonstration in which a group of activists go to the homes or workplaces of those whom they want to condemn and publicly humiliate in order to influence decision makers) and public mockery of the "Degenerated" works.

An exhibition of the "Degenerated Art" was made (they called it Modern Art) where different Nazis gave lectures to criticize these Artists and disqualify them considering them a destructive trend. The reflection aimed to mobilize race consciousness and purge these conspiring elements so that the German people are oppressed. All this to neutralize these evil influences that pursued the defeat of the collective "Aryan race" against other groups that wanted their oppression and destruction.

It is interesting, both in Nazis and in feminazis, that acts of book burning are carried out and also attacks on artists.

Recently John William Waterhouse's "Hylas and the Nymphs" was temporarily removed from the Manchester Art Gallery, because it perpetuated "harmful stories" about women and girls, depicting them either as decorative objects or femme fatales. This work depicts a pond full of naked water nymphs imploring a young man to join them for a swim.

The Museum authorities (feminazis) held that their decision was, in itself, an artistic fact.

Is the political fact, then, an artistic fact? Interestingly (or not so much), it is the same theory that Goebbels, the Propaganda Minister of Nazi Germany, had.

According to Goebbels, the political fact is an artistic fact. Is the claim of these bureaucrats correct - to give themselves the title of Artists - for exercising power authoritatively?

Goebbels dreamed of being an Artist and was an admirer of the German writer Herman Hesse. Hesse cultivated the genre of the initiation novel. In imitation of his hero Hesse, the young Goebbels wrote an initiation novel called "Michael", where he exposed his theory of politician as an artist.

Thus, Michael, Goebbels' character, said: *"The mass is like stone to the sculptor. Leader and mass, the relationship is exactly as little problematic as, for example, the one between painter and sculptor. Politics is the plastic art of the State in the same way that painting is the painter's plastic art,* "said Goebbels in that novel.

However ... Is the politician an artist as these authoritarians and censors claim?

In our opinion the politician's logic is different from the Art logic.

The politician's logic is to reproduce the discourse that serves his goal of having power (for example, the bureaucrats of the Manchester Museum by demonstrating "gender perspective" and censor Waterhouse, they do the "politically correct" and increase their power, they joined the "metoo" movement), the politician repeats the speech of the other, while the logic of the Artist is to express his most genuine part, the most genuine gives the originality

Goebbels could never be Herman Hesse. Herman Hesse said "*Who doesn't fit in this world, it's closer to find himself*"

Hesse didn't fit in Nazi Germany, because he didn't say the fashion speech. Herman Hesse was not a politician, he was an Artist. Instead, Goebbels changed his ideas, changed his convictions, in order to adapt them to what was convenient for his goal of promotion. Goebbels was a bureaucrat, a person without convictions that adapts to the ideology of the moment (as are the censorship authorities of the Manchester Museum).

The Artist is more misfit, the politician is more hypocritical.

The "conversion" of Goebbels to racism is very interesting.

Before his political career took flight, Goebbels had a girlfriend of Jewish origin. She was very good to him in his worst moments of unemployment, frustration and depression (he even got him a job at the Bank), but, in order to satisfy Hitler's ideas, he left her when his political career gained importance.

But his ideological conversion is interesting. For that, we can think of three classes of collectivist (Hegel followers)

a) those who are fighting for class

b) those who are fighting for races

c) those who are fighting for gender.

The three have in common to play the card of "The Victim" and present themselves as members of a collective (good) that is victimized by the other (bad), but, in addition, the three have in common the idea of conspiracy, of anteroom

Goebbels, as a Hegelian of the class struggle, belonged to the most left wing of the

Nazi Party. They were suspicious of the "bourgeois ideas" of the Munich circle, which was the officers surrounding Hitler in the districts of Southern Germany. As a Hegelian of the class struggle with conspiratorial dyes, Goebbels believed that Hitler's racism was part of the "superstructure", was a part of the conspiracy of the oppressive collective (the bourgeoisie) to victimize the oppressed collective (the working class) and that Don't wake up to "class consciousness."

However, Hitler, Hegelian but of the races, presented him with another type of conspiracy and another type of victimization. He told him that Marxism was part of the "Jewish conspiracy" so that the oppressed collective (the Aryan race) does not see the secret oppression carried out by the oppressive collective. So the interesting thing is that both theories fight and throw their conspiratorial poison at each other; Nazism accuses Marxism of being part of the Jewish conspiracy so that there is no race consciousness, but, for its part, Marxism accuses Nazism of being part of the bourgeois conspiracy so that there is no class consciousness; Feminazism could accuse the previous two of being part of the patriarchal conspiracy so that there is no "gender perspective".

In all three cases, the victim's role and the idea of conspiracy are widely used. However, Goebbels, an intelligent, trained person with a university degree, was not allowed to "convince" by Hitler, but his ideological transformation obeyed the logic of the politician. The politician is a climber, the politician adapts, the politician fits into the world.

Hitler, as part of his meteoric career to power, needed to loosen the anti-bourgeois discourse of the Northern Nazis, because part of his success was the german industrialists financial support. So, rewarding Goebbels with a lot of prominence and in a seduction operation, he dragged him towards his ideological turn. The co-religionists of Goebbels, the Nazis of the North, seeing their claudication, called this process the "Damascus of Joseph Goebbels", when he ceased to be a furious hater of the bourgeois conspirator and became an equally racist furious.

It is not true what Goebbels and the Manchester Museum authorities say: they are not Artists, they are politicians, they are climbers, they renounce their convictions to adapt to the discourse of the moment that serves to accommodate them, they are parrots that repeat the Fashion idea of the moment.

Just as Goebbels, to be able to climb, he stopped being a Hegelian of the class struggle and became a Hegelian of the race struggle ... we have no doubt: if today Goebbels lived he would be a Hegelian of the gender struggle, Goebbels if wake up in the 21st century would become feminazi. He was a bureaucrat, someone who adapts to the fashion idea of the moment.

On the other hand, the curious idea shared by Goebbels and the authorities of the Manchester Museum (the idea of political fact as an artistic fact) deserves further reflection. Maybe it deserves a whole book of reflections.

If the political fact is an artistic fact, then ... people are not people, but part of an inert mass that the politician manipulates. The authorities of the Manchester Museum do not let the museum visitors see the painting ... Why? Why not let the visitors of the Manchester Museum see the painting and, in any case, if Waterhouse is "patriarchal", the same visitors can think for themselves and have their own conclusion? Why do these censors believe that people are stupid, that people cannot judge for themselves a work of art?

The answer lies in collectivism, these types of bureaucrats do not see you as a person capable of thinking for themselves, but as part of a "mass", as part of a "collective." If they believe they are sculptors and that people are "the sculptor's stone" as Goebbels said, then they treat the public as if it were an inanimate object, because they cannot think for themselves.

Marxists, Nazis and Feminazis are intrinsically authoritarian and censors, because they see people as an inanimate mass, unable to think for themselves.

Besides ... Why do we find these ideological brothers, ideological children of Hegel, in the same place?

Why do we find them censor the Artists?

To find an answer, one must think that they - in their ideological base - also owe a lot to Nietzsche. As tributaries of Nietzsche, they have distrust of Culture. Culture is so powerful that it can drag people towards their destruction. Culture ... is something to distrust from their eyes. The feminazis took from Freud and Freud took Nietzsche.

Cultural impositions, Culture, according to Nietzsche, can move the human being away from his animal nature, the Judeo-Christian culture, according to Nietzsche, has corrupted the human being, has removed him from his bestiality.

There is a dichotomy between "instincts" and "culture," where culture can imprison the human being, can take away his instincts, can tame him according to Nietzsche.

In Nietzsche, culture is the Judeo-Christian "Slave Moral" that corrupted people and took them away from their instincts.

Betty Friedman, in the book "The Feminine Mystique" criticizes Freud, but the influence of Freud and Nietzsche is obvious. The author, essentially, reproaches Freud (and therefore Nietzsche) for not having contemplated the victimization of women by Culture. This "Mystique" is an oppressive entity that lives in the Culture, it is the concept of feminine that is in the Culture, but the author reifies it, then the "voices of the Culture" that make force for the Woman don't be free.

In addition, Nazis and Feminazis also, in their ideological foundations, owe Karl Marx. It was Marx who argued that Culture could be part of the disguise that the oppressor group wore so that the oppressed group cannot warn of secret victimization. For Marx, culture is part of the so-called "superstructure," the Marxist superstructure is made up of religion, ideologies such as nationalism, culture in general. The superstructure is a varnish, a disguise, secretly put by the bourgeois class so that the working class cannot awaken the "class consciousness." Culture is part of the Conspiracy.

In the Nazis, the "Degenerated Culture" is also a secret scheme of the "inferior races" to prevent the "superior race" from reaching its destination of greatness. The Nazis' obsession with Culture - he saw in Culture part of the imagined conspiracy - led them to absurd decisions, such as the entire ban on music styles. The so-called "national socialist revolution" then forbade, for example, Jazz. Jazz was a degenerate music secretly played by the lower races to oppress and harm the superior race.

In fact, radicalized feminist groups come to influence the Education programs to try to indoctrinate the next generations with the "gender ideology".

-VI- THE FIVE CHARACTERISTICS OF THE SOCIAL PSYCHOLOGY OF FEMINAZIS AND OF ALL IDEOLOGIES OF HATE.

When the American communicator Rush Limbaught used the word "Feminazi" to refer to these fanatic movements that fight against an imaginary Patriarchy, the term immediately was welcomed by millions of people.

It was an impeccable definition - from the intuitive and conceptual - to designate to these forms of the psychology of "hatred of the different", of paranoia and of the epic, covered with some intellectual contributions of Hegelian collectivist origin. They did not like it and, with their natural authoritarianism, tried to ban it, but more and more people started using it. That is good, because if many people use the term "Feminazi", it means that there are social antibodies to reject the ideologies of hatred, of the stereotype, of discrimination that justify an extremely aggressive position just as presented as "The Victim."

Therefore, the word Feminazi is much more adequate and descriptive than "Female chauvinist" to refer to these groups.

Beyond the accusations that we can all receive for contradicting these authoritarian people, we continue with the study of this very correct concept - in its descriptive force - to represent the phenomenon.

Now we can make a portrait of the 5 characteristics of Nazi Social Psychology. These 5 points in common are the most important because the intellectual part has no value (both Nazis and Feminazis have unsupported ideas, very silly ... they are due to Hegel, but they did not read it), the important thing is the underlying psychological causes.

THE 5 CHARACTERISTICS

1- Draw a division to people according to some personal characteristic (it can be good race / bad race, good gender / bad gender, good religion / bad religion, nationals / foreigners, etc.) to generate forced collectives and then raise a victimization, by establishing that there is an "oppressive group" and an "oppressed group".

2 - Make a comparison between the two groups that is beneficial for the self-esteem of the "oppressed group" and the detrimental to the self-esteem of the "oppressor group", trying to give human attributes to the oppressed

group and dehumanize the oppressor group. Disgust towards the oppressive group is also encouraged in order to cut empathy.

3- Describe the oppressor group as an extremely powerful force. This is very important, because the epic appeal is achieved only with the battle of powerful enemies and this appeal is decisive to give euphoric emotional attraction to the "Fight."

4- Raise a conspiracy that bids to carry out the oppression in a secret way so that the oppressed never realize what is happening.

5-Attribute deaths to the secret and evil actions of the oppressive group, so that vindictive violence against any other person is justified, since, in this rhetoric, individuals are not individuals (unique, unrepeatable, with unique life stories), but "Representatives of its collective".

1- Draw a division to people according to some personal characteristic to form groups.

Jessa Crispin, in a book entitled "Why I Am Not a Feminist" concludes "*It is always easier to find your sense of value by demeaning another's value. It is easier to define yourself as 'not that,' rather than do an actual accounting of your own qualities and put them on the scale*"

That is precisely what a psychological theory widely used in science studies to understand the social psychology of prejudice, discrimination, violence and stereotypes.

It is the Social Identity Theory of Tajfel and Turner.

The theory explains that part of a person's concept of self comes from the groups to which that person belongs. An individual does not just have a personal selfhood, but multiple selves and identities associated with their affiliated groups.

There are three processes that create this <u>ingroup</u>/ outgroup mentality

a) Categorization.

The first is categorization. We categorize objects in order to understand them and identify them. In a very similar way we categorize people (including ourselves) in order to understand the social environment.

The categories can be white, black, German, student, fan of such football club, worker, national or immigrant, etc. By categorizing individuals, oneself can find the category to which it belongs (the ingroup) and recognize those who, because they do not have that characteristic, do not belong (the outgroup).

b) Identification

After this, people identify with the groups to which they believe they belong. The identification carries with it two results. Part of who we are is governed by the group we belong to, sometimes we think like "we" and sometimes like "me". By thinking of "we" as members of a group, our social identity is defined.

c) Comparison.

Then we see the members of our group as "people" and we tend to dehumanize the members of the outgroup (those who do not have the characteristic that makes us a group). Then we reinforce our self-esteem as a group by comparing ourselves to the outgroup and insulting it.

This theory of social psychology begins to help explain the psychology of the appeal of ideas such as Nazism or Feminazism. It is about choosing a characteristic of any person to divide them into groups (race in one case, gender in the other), after that identify as part of a group ("race" in one case, "gender "In the other) and finally establish a comparison of our group with the other that tends to dehumanize the other, to strengthen our self-esteem in a group ("

death to the lower races "in one case," death to the male "in the other).

In this comparison of the ingroup with the outgroup, these extreme ideologies aim not only to exalt the group itself and denigrate the other, but also to dehumanize the members of the outgroup.

Many times feminazis manage to pressure to leave unemployed women who work with their beauty, such as hostesses, models. They make demonstrations to end fashion shows, under threat of accusing brands of "male chauvinist." Is it a coincidence that so many beautiful women lose a space where they could be recognized and a possibility of work such as parades and beauty pageants? No, it is not. In Feminazism there is also Envy, Envy is a suffering that decreases when it is possible to despise the merit of others.

Therefore, if at first the envious woman suffers for the beauty of her rival, then, thanks to feminazism, she can despise her and, thus, lower the suffering of envy. Thanks to feminazism, that same woman who once took all eyes, who had the body that produced so much anger, can be seen as a "poor manified by the Patriarchy", and, the formerly envious sufferer, look at herself as a enlightened that "deconstructed" her identity of the patriarchal construction and that, now, from this new and gratifying superiority, she can try to take work from the pretty woman in the name of the latter's good, since the feminine has a higher consciousness, to be "deconstructed".

If, as an individual, it was difficult for him to support his identity on his personal merits, through the story of two groups (one victim and another oppressor), the feminazi can have a much better social identity and, thus, abandon a self-account that It left her at a disadvantage compared to other women. So Social Identity, the process of abandoning all individuality and categorizing as part of a group, is important especially if you have a lot of personal resentment.

<u>2- Make a comparison between the own group (ingroup) and the foreign group (outgroup). Dehumanize the outgroup and generate Disgust. Accusing the outgroup of victimizing the ingroup</u>.

These ideologies of hate serve, in the first instance, to increase self-esteem, because by merging as part of a collective, then comparisons can be made with the other collective and thus highlight one's identity.

In radical feminism, the outgroup (males) is usually compared to animals such as monkeys and pigs, in order to also reaffirm humanity as an exclusivity of the ingroup (females). To see this, you can read various feminazis books , but one of the most representative is SCUM Manifesto.Society for Cutting Up Men Valerie Solanas.

"The male is by his very nature, a leech, an emotional parasite, an therefore, not ethically entitled to live".

"Just as humans have a prior right to existence over dogs by virtue of being more highly evolved and having a superior consciousness, so women have a prior right to existence over men. The elimination of any male is, therefore, a righteous and good act, an act highly beneficial to women as well as an act of mercy"

The word "Leech" that Solanas uses to describe the outgroup ("men") is very effective discursively to represent the theory of the two groups, the "oppressed group" and the "oppressor group", precisely because the "Leech" is an aggressive bug that takes advantage of the other to survive. The oppressed group would be the women and the oppressive group "the leeches" that survive by attacking the former.

In addition, to support prejudice, Repulsion is a very important emotion.

Indeed, the greatest experts in aggression and discrimination have seen the importance of Repugnance as to allow cruelty.

The philosopher Marta Nussbaum, for example, is interested in "Disgust" as a limit to moral compassion

According to the author, we extend to other human beings the idea that they are disgusting objects that should not be close to us. Repugnance is emotion - says the author - that precedes hatred and humiliation and has been the cause of great evils for humanity.

An example of this "Disgust" we would have in the example of "The Untouchables" in India. The Untouchables are the lowest link in the castes of India; They perform functions such as cleaning the feces of the richest families in exchange for food. According to these traditions, touching an "untouchable" or its objects is a sign of pollution and unworthiness. After touching an "untouchable" a series of purification rituals is necessary to return to a normal state.

Nussbaum in "*Hiding from Humanity: Disgust, Shame, and the Law*" speaks of a natural history of shame and humiliation as a narrative of the deepest causes by which human societies, again and again, seek to mark the faces of some of their members, which leads to live with a "stained identity." The people in question *"are crawling, not on par with others in terms of human dignity."*

These "marked" people cause a distance from others, who feel they must be at a distance so as not to contaminate their disgust. . Nussbaum argues that the thought-content of disgust embodies *"magical ideas of contamination, and impossible aspirations to purity that are just not in line with human life as we know it"*

In the texts of radical feminists, not only do they usually compare men with aggressive animals (to victimize themselves), but with filthy animals, to generate disgust towards the group.

Within the scenario that the Feminazi ideology portrays, where people are necessarily seen as parts of a group, give humanity to the members of the ingroup (people with the characteristics of being women) and take humanity from the members of the outgroup and associate them with leeches, It is very effective for all these purposes:

a) dehumanize them

b) state that they are aggressive and that the ingroup is a victim of them

c) describe them with a repulsive animal, to cause disgust and less compassion.

The Nazis used such comparisons with rats, leeches, pigs or other bugs that arouse disgust (see, among other examples, Hitler's speech of August 13, 1920).

In the speeches of extreme feminism this can often be seen in the dehumanization of men.

The dehumanization of the male is achieved from comparison with animals, but animals that are aggressive - to victimize - and that serve to generate disgust.

Therefore, the pig, being a dirty animal, is often chosen for this comparison ("male chauvinist pig")

In addition, it is no accident that people who have the characteristic of being male, are called "males."

This word, the word "Male" and its derivations, is central to feminazis and is not accidental, because it aims to link th eoutgroup with the animal kingdom, because dehumanizing the other is a necessary step in this type of hate ideologies.

They do not define themselves as "females" in their songs. But, to the outgroup, instead, they are called "Males", the differentiated rhetorical procedure aims to compare a group of humans (the ingroup, the women) and a dehuman group, consisting of animals (the outgroup, the "males") .

The allusion to the "Dirt" of the "Males" is a constant reason also, to increase the Disgust.

*"Every man, deep down, knows he's a worthless piece of shit."*Valerie Solanas

"To call a man an animal is to flatter him; he's a machine, a walking dildo. It's often said that men use women. Use them for what ?Surely not pleasure." Valerie Solanas.

Flo Kennedy called Solanas *"ones of the most important spokeswoman for the feminist movement"* in her long introduction to the 1970 edition of the "Scum Manifesto" and Vivian Gornkik called Solanas a *"visionary"* who *"understood the true nature of the struggle for women s liberation."*

Gornik's statement is false, because feminists must be differentiated from feminazis, but it is true that Solanas reveals the true feelings of feminazis

Now, it would be silly to compare Valerie Solanas with Hitler, but the social reaction to such texts is important.

According to all historians, Hitler was taken to grace by the people of his time during the 20s. He was a comic character, they went to the breweries to listen to an extreme hate speech as fun and without ever taking it too much seriously.

A man shouting with grandiloquent gestures that politicians had to be shot, to establish a racist state and a dictatorship, was all so extreme that he looked funny and, thus, called attention. He has even referred to Hitler's social perception rather as a quirky comic character, a funny figure for his extremism.

It is taken to grace, as if it were a "satire" and when Solanas proposes that men are leeches that must be exterminated in the "gas chamber", various feminist blogs repeat it and celebrate as if it were something fun.

In any case, these "authentic feminist feelings" revealed by the SCUM Manifesto are those that underlie the current Courts of Justice that have a "gender perspective"

The sentences of the Feminazi Courts would be unfair to the naked eye - for unequal treatment - but they are understood if men are dehumanized: dehumanizing justifies cruelty and discrimination.

"The man who is extremely and dangerously hungry has no other interest but food. Capacities not useful for the satisfying of hunger are pushed into the background. 'But what happens to man's desires when there is plenty of food and his belly in chronically filled? At once, other (and higher) needs emerge and these, rather than the psychological hungers, dominate the organism."" Betty Friedan

"At least three further requirements supplement the strategies of environmentalists if we were to create and preserve a less violent world. 1) Every culture must begin to affirm the female future. 2) Species responsibility must be returned to women in every culture. 3) The proportion of men must be reduced to and maintained at approximately ten percent of the human race." Sally Miller Gearhart.

"If life is to survive on this planet, there must be a decontamination of the Earth. I think this will be accompanied by an evolutionary process that will result in a drastic reduction of the population of males" Mary Daly.

Various authors insist on depriving men of more mental attributes (such as culture, emotions, sensibility, ideas) to dehumanize them and represent them as dangerous animals that, if they do not want food, want sex. Instead, women (the ingroup) reserves all of humanity.

According to the Social Identity Theory, these stereotypes between the "ingroup" and the "outgroup" are fundamental, because they allow a simplified view of "The Others".

In all cases, the subjects of the outgroup are not returned as individuals, but as "part of a group" (the oppressor group) and under the prejudice that all were equal.

Nick Haslam (2006), reviewing the research on dehumanization of the other, concludes that there are two most common ways of dehumanizing. Compare the other with machines and compare it with animals.

For Lasana Harris and Susan Fiske (2009), there is a relationship between the dehumanized perception of others and the attributes of low warmth and low ability. The authors state that dehumanization is accompanied by the emotion of disgust.

Therefore, all these hate ideologies not only use aggressive animals to describe the enemy collective, but also they choose animals that raise disgust, such as rats, worms, pigs, leeches, etc.

3- Represent the outgroup as a very powerful force.

This type of ideology states that our "group" (necessarily put us in a group, although we do not want, by some characteristic, sex, race, religion, skin color, nationality) is the victim of an oppressive and harmful action from the other "group." This victimization tries to attribute to the group indicated as oppressor very serious, shameful, cruel acts.

Why monstrous powers? Because fighting a powerful enemy is more feat than fighting a weak enemy. Narcissism, pride, vanity is what clouds our reason and makes us believe in these ideas.

In this regard, the "feats" are those that increase our pride. For example, it is more feat to climb an Everest than to climb a dune (Taken from "The M.A.S and the M.A.P .: a psychological theory, Martin Ross).

Difficulty enhances the feat a lot.

But for all these objectives to be achieved, it is important that belonging is a feat, so that belonging to the struggle is a feat, then the dialectical enemy (no matter if it is an invented enemy) cannot be weak.

If they faced a weak enemy ... How could it be an epic fight?

On the contrary, the imaginary enemy, The Patriarchy, is extremely powerful, it is evil, but above all things it is Powerful, infinitely Powerful.

Then it is about inventing an imaginary enemy linked to the outgroup that is so powerful that it generates the battle epic. Because the measure of the power of the enemy is the measure of the epic, describing the imaginary enemy as very powerful is important to believe the heroism of the fight.

The imaginary enemy is so but so powerful that those who profess these hate ideologies like to show themselves as desperate

David who face super-powerful Goliaths, as very brave people.

These types of ideas tend to represent their enemy in a way so but so powerful and threatening that, if for a second it were accepted that this representation is true, then it would be seen as a true epic struggle.

As the basis of adherence to these movements is pride, euphoria, epic and it is important to describe a super-powerful enemy.

4-The conspiracy.

The fourth element is the "Conspiracy." It is one of the most important elements.

This type of ideology always uses the conspiracy component that implies that there are two realities: a) the facade (which is what the naked eye can see) b) the conspiracy, where the powerful and evil conspirators take precautions so that no one discovers their Secret action to harm the ingroup.

Feminazism, like Marxism - two sons of Hegel - uses the conspiracy idea a lot, the idea of the "Veil", the idea that evil entities (cultural abstractions) hide their actions.

Therefore, feminazis are created in the center of a spiral of "Higher Consciousness" that allows them to look at other women with contempt, because they are in the circles of lesser "Consciousness." For women, the other women are "built" - and do not know it - by this conspiracy to achieve their submission and vexation and only they have "deconstructed" to reach this enlightened state of Consciousness Supremacy.

"It is interesting that many women do not recognize themselves as discriminated against; no better proof could be found of the totality of their conditioning." Kate Millett, Sexual Politics

Conspiracy theories usually go against a general consensus or one that cannot be proven using the historical method. They are based on the fact that actors "out of the picture, in secret" and with great power execute actions with unethical purposes to achieve hidden objectives, often causing disastrous effects.

Thus, one can speak of many conspiracy theories. The dominion of the reptilians, the hegemony of the Illuminati, the false arrival of the man to the Moon recorded in a study, the truth about the attacks of 9/11, the false death of Elvis or the death and replacement of Paul McCartney

According to Kent University psychologists Michael J. Wood, Karen M. Douglas and Robbie M. Sutton in a publication titled Dead and Alive: Beliefs in Contradictory Conspiracy Theories, a conspiracy theory is *"a proposed plot by powerful people or organizations working together in secret to accomplish some (usually sinister) goal"*.

Once you believe that *"one massive, sinister conspiracy could be successfully executed in near-perfect secrecy it suggests that many such plots are possible."*

You can also understand the seduction that conspiracy theories exert under the *Shield Feat Theory,* a theory that relates conspiratorial beliefs to the persecutory delusions of paranoids and psychotics.

The "shield feat" would be a process to protect against potential anti-feat. Given the vulnerability caused by a risk of anti-feat (personal situation of defeat, shame, derision), the shield feat becomes a bumper that serves to better withstand it.

One of the most important shield feats is the pessimistic shield feat of "awareness" that could be used for conspiracy theories.

Under this logic, if an unbearable defeat or shame is going to happen to us, if, at least "we are aware".

It may be the case of those who fear being disapproved in an exam and that causes a lot of anguish, says "I will disapprove" and, if that finally happens, says "At least, I was aware"

An example of a shield feat may be that of the jealous who accuses his partner that he was unfaithful. So, if he is really unfaithful, he has an early compensation when he can say "At least, I was aware" (See Shield Feats Theory, Martin Ross).

In paranoid delusions, the paranoid has too much psychic vulnerability to the anti-feat of being defeated and defeated by those imaginary enemies. Then, to have a consolation prize if this happens, "He aware" that his enemies attack him so that, if his defeat finally arrives, he can say "I realized, I'm not so dumb, I already knew."

Therefore, in the event that our reputation were to suffer the blow of a very powerful anti-feat (so powerful that it will destroy all prestige and personal pride forever), the "Awareness" of it will be an early compensation that will allow us Improve the final balance.

Suspicion, suspicion is characteristic of the pre-psychotic state: in the face of the vulnerability of being able to suffer an anti-feat, "Awareness" the hidden, the secret, it can be a perceptual ability that compensates for the final balance, an anticipated merit that is searched in reserve.

A conspiracy theory, questions us because it tells us that we are being victims of a warp maneuver not only to harm us, but, above all, to be able to deceive us. In every conspiracy theory, there is a staging, since it is always a group of people with evil intent who make a secret plan for us to believe in something that is not true.

Therefore, the act of "not believing" in conspiracy theory exposes us to the risk of succumbing to the conspirators' deception and doing exactly what they want: not to aware their secret actions. Instead, the shield feat of "awareness" leads us to "Believe" in the alleged conspiracy.

"Believe" even if we don't have rational elements to support that belief. In this way, our self-esteem is protected from any possibility of deception, if we "believe" in the conspiracy there is no way that we are taking the risk of being deceived by the conspirators.

According to the Theory of Shield Feats, then, the success of conspiracy ideas is that large layers of the population, given a story of these characteristics, choose "Believe" in the existence of the conspiracy, rather than not for lack of evidence.

In the feminine descriptions of reality this "anteroom" of the conspirators is always verified (the conspirators are the patriarchal culture and The Patriarchy).

For example, a typical Feminazi reflection could be like this *"They told us that fairy tales where the prince kissed a princess and the princess woke up, were naive stories, but they never told us that, with those stories, gender stereotypes were intended so that the woman learns to be submissive"*.

When someone can ask you, with a touch of wisdom, do you want to convince me that the people who invented those stories were thinking about how to cheat women to format their heads and make them submissive to macho oppression? The answer could be to invoke abstract entities, such as attributing to the evil Patriarchy to have induced the generation of these tales, by influencing - secretly - the minds of the creators of these stories.

Pablo Neruda wrote a verse that begins "I like for you to be still: it is as though you were absent, and you hear me from far away and my voice does not touch you." And feminazis see two things there: a) the facade (a romantic verse) b) the hidden anteroom, a propaganda of the Patriarchy to inoculate the woman with the message that she has to shut up.

The idea of conspiracy and an evil power behind that digits a false facade in the media is very present in this type of ideas.

A frequent delirium in schizophrenia is the idea that we have "implanted" our thoughts and that we are being watched and spied on. Strange forces drive us by implanting outside thoughts. The problem of habitual individual psychoses is that they have a very precarious rational basis, because the psychotic does not always find to give good intellectual foundations to his own delirium and, therefore, many times, to be able to believe in his delirium, the psychotic uses disorganized or bizarre thoughts.

However, another thing is a seductive idea to realize a collective delirium, even if it is the same psychological basis, the collective delirium - the fanatic sect, Nazism, radical feminism - can have a much greater intellectual support.

This can be achieved with oppressive imaginary entities - covered by conspiratorial elements so as not to be visible - that are to blame for all our frustrations, imaginary abstract entities such as "The Patriarchy."

*"Society, being codified by man, decrees that woman is inferior; she can do away with this inferiority only by destroying the male's superiority "*Simone de Beauvoir.

"The fact is that men encounter more complicity in their woman companions than the oppressor usually finds in the oppressed; and in bad faith they use it as a pretext to declare that

woman wanted the destiny they imposed on her. We have seen that in reality her whole education conspires to bar her from paths of revolt and adventure; all of society - beginning with her respected parents - lies to her in extolling the high value of love, devotion, and the gift of self and in concealing the fact that neither lover, husband nor children will be disposed to bear the burdensome responsibility of it. She cheerfully accepts these lies because they invite her to take the easy slope: and that is the worst of the crimes committed against her; from her childhood and throughout her life, she is spoiled, she is corrupted by the fact that this resignation, tempting to any existent anxious about her freedom, is mean to be her vocation; if one encourages a child to be lazy by entertaining him all day, without giving him the occasion to study, without showing him its value, no one will say when he reaches the age of man that he chose to be incapable and ignorant; this is how the woman is raised, without ever being taught the necessity of assuming her own existence; she readily lets herself count on the protection, love, help and guidance of others; she lets herself be fascinated by the hope of being able to realise her being without doing anything. She is wrong to yield to this temptation; but the man is ill advised to reproach her for it since it is he himself who tempted her" Simone de Beauvoir

As you can see, the hypothetical wife described by De Beauvoir is a victim of a conspiracy of actors who pretend not to "warn" him, because his parents, husband and lover are synchronized in lying to prevent the roads of rebellion. The author, with this text, reveals to her reader "the conspiracy", runs the curtain, and shows the reality that was hidden.

5- Attribute deaths to the outgroup and horrific crimes.

The invention of "Femicide" serves to feminazis appropriate the dead, to make them their own, to serve their ideological cause of being able to blame the entire outgroup. Thus feminazis appropriate the deaths, make them their own.

Another invention is "gender violence." It refers to violence against women, *Due to the fact of being women and practiced by men*", especially by the cultural canons of a "patriarchal" society.

This does not exist. It's stupid. It was never proved - with scientific evidence - that some forms of domestic violence are due to these determinants.

Although there is no gender-based violence, it is ideologically necessary to charge the entire outgroup with responsibility for the crimes of the murderers, within a Hegelian account of opposing groups, where one group occupies the role of oppressor and the other group the oppressed.

In addition, the very serious violence attributed to the demonized collective justifies giving moral authority to the epic struggle.

Conclusions

In general, this tendency of people to renounce their individual identity and build their identity with a group characteristic (nationality, sex, skin color, religion, etc.) to reinforce their own superiority with the denigration of the outgroup, is characteristic of Very resentful people. Only the most frustrated, most resentful individuals can find great seduction in this type of ideas to channel their anger, find super-powerful culprits and feel much better when they feel victimized.

For these reasons of social psychology, so many women hate "inclusive language". It is that they are women who, rather than women, feel "Individual and Unique People" and do not accept to be pigeonholed with the script of members of an alleged "victimized collective". They do not feel victims and the inclusive language - that authoritarian invention used to make propaganda is intended to give them that place necessarily, so they reject it.

Those who have individual merits, they feel unique people, they feel different from "the mass", they reject the ideologies that seek to give them the quality of "victimized collective", they are people before any "belonging".

On the other hand, when a person cannot find fulfillment in their personal life history, they may find it better to feel part of "an oppressed group" and channel their anger and frustration in a comparison with the "oppressiveoutgroup" that tends towards violence and towards the stigmatization of the other.

Although this dialectical and binary representation of the world between "oppressive group" and "oppressed group" has no evidence, conspiracy theories can be used to neutralize any evidence against it.

The reasons of social psychology that have been described here are those that underlie the process and determine it, but they are covered with the ideological reasons that come from irrationalist philosophers such as Hegel, Foucault and Nietzsche where a dialectic appears between "oppressive group" and "group oppressed "covered with conspiracy theory and distrust towards Culture with a vocation of censorship.

All this gives rise to the Feminazi movement.

The best way to recognize a Feminazi is that she uses the word "Patriarchy", a dialectical and super-powerful imaginary entity that gives his imaginary "Fight" epic character.

-VII- THE NEW FEMINAZIS COURTS.

The lie of "gender violence" consists in identifying, within all forms of domestic violence, some of whom the political and ideological decision is made to call it that.

There is no evidence of "gender violence." It's a fantasy.

It is impossible that there is scientific evidence, because "gender violence" is another brick in a conceptual tower of a building built on the foundations of Hegel, a philosopher who criticizes the reason

Indeed, the "gender violence" construct is based on postmodern currents of thought that are "Anti-Realistic." Then show that there is an objective reality to describe, all are speeches, all are political positions.

On the contrary, any claim to scientific evidence can be comfortably disqualified by postmodernists by saying something like this: "You ask me for evidence from the capitalist discourse of science, which has claims of neutrality, which is positivist, but I have another position".

In other words: there is no scientific evidence that gender violence exists, nor do they intend to give it and can even disqualify anyone who asks for evidence.

Gender violence means violence induced by the patriarchal macho culture, the violence exerted by an oppressive collective (men), over an oppressed group (women) by following the secret design of an imaginary cultural entity called "The Patriarchy" .

For example, United Nations gives this definition:

"The terms 'gender-based violence' and 'violence against women' are frequently used interchangeably in literature and by advocates, however, the term gender-based violence refers to violence directed against a person because of his of her gender and expectations of his or her role in a society or culture. Gender-based violence highlights the gender dimension of these types of acts; in other words, the relationship between females' subordinate status in society and their increased vulnerability to violence. It is important to note, however, that men and boys may also be victims of gender-based violence, especially sexual violence".

And Gender Violence defines it as*"Violence that results in, or is likely to result in, physical, sexual or psychological harm or suffering, against someone based on gender discrimination, gender role expectations and/or* *gender stereotypes, or based on the differential power status linked to gender"*.

Of course, we recognize that there is domestic violence and violence in general.

What we are trying is another hypothesis: that there are people who kill by order of the villain king who lives in the culture "The Patriarchy".

They are not really saying that the murderer makes all the reasoning ("*this woman does not adapt to the stereotypes of the Patriarchy, ergo I have the right to kill her*"), but that - supposedly - it would be something unconscious, the unconscious influence of culture patriarchal who predisposes, pushes, the oppressors to exercise it on the oppressed.

Gender violence occurs when the violent acts, then, as the arm of the oppressive Patriarchy.

Now: How the hell did they prove that there is a man - one alone - who believed in patriarchal gender stereotypes, who followed the tacit dictates of the Patriarchy and who, under all these circumstances, exercised violence and even murdered?

They did not prove it. It is not scientific.

In fact, scientific research warns of the pitiful "political" and not "scientific" approach that government violence programs have in couples. These state programs are influenced by the theory - devoid of evidence - of the "Patriarchy" and this conspires against its effectiveness to achieve more effective interventions. It is emphasized that it is important to remove ideology and use the evidence. (See, for example, Louise Dixon and colleagues, 2012).

What is the important and political implication of these concepts without scientific evidence? Why is it so important to call some murderers "femicides" and not just murderers?

The invention of gender violence has many implications:

a) it provides epic arguments and moral authority to the feminazis to carry out their struggle against the imaginary Patriarchy, because femicide is that homicidal who kills as a Patriarchy soldier

b) this concept manages to blame all the members of the oppressive group (people with the characteristic of being men) of the deaths.

From there, it is how the reversal of the burden of proof is installed in Criminal Law and in the Courts of Justice.

We are no longer an Individualist Justice that judges people. We have a Hegelian Justice that judges collectives.

Who is male then integrates the "oppressive collective" and, therefore, "is guilty."

For the Feminazi Justice there are no men as individual persons, but an oppressive group that must be punished to level in this dialectical confrontation between the oppressor group and the oppressed group, according to the theory of Patriarchy.

Men accused of gender-based violence are "guilty" The violation of the minimum guarantees that make criminal law is understood because the liberal criminal law - which judges individuals- is replaced by a new Hegelian law of collectives -which judges collectives-

Every man is partly guilty of all the murders of women, even if he is more peaceful than Gandhi. Every man is guilty from the perspective of the Feminazis Courts, he is guilty because he is not seen as a singular person, but as a representative of an oppressive collective that leads in that Collective Justice the dialectical confrontation with the oppressed collective.

Filing a complaint about "gender violence" by a woman is the fastest and safest way to ensure that a) the exclusive use of the home is guaranteed b) the custody of her children c) money. If the complaint is false that does not change the effects at all, because the presumption of the evidence is reversed.

In practice, it translates into hundreds of thousands of children who remain without seeing their parents for decades, criminal convictions for "gender violence" without evidence, men who lose their homes or are imprisoned for hundreds of thousands of false allegations . It must be borne in mind that, from the eyes of Hegel and (and, therefore, of one of his children, feminazis), individual rights would be very secondary.

In this case, the oppressed group ("women") implements their revenge on the oppressive group ("men"), and individual stories - for example, of a baby who is left without seeing the father - are irrelevant.

The problem is that the Law is something concrete and real, the person who loses his house for a sentence based on gender ideology does not see it as "post-truth", but as something concrete and real. The child who remains 10 years without seeing his father for a judicial decision without evidence based on gender ideology, does not see it as "Possession" or as an entelechy of irrationalist speeches, but something very specific in his personal and concrete life. The gender ideology - which is characterized by reducing social and political reality to a dialectical struggle between the group considered oppressed "women" and the oppressive collective, "men" - is nourished by Hegel, but also by the Hegelian Marx

These new gender courts are an opportunity to have a good job. You must repeat "Patriarchy", take courses and postgraduate courses on "gender perspective" to get to have a public office. They are the courses of "gender violence" where the key is to acquire a pompous language, say words such as "post-truth", a language full of reifications, and often repeat the word "gender perspective". People want to change the car, go on vacation to a nice place, pay their children's schools and, for those practical purposes, it is an objective to occupy one of these courts.

-VIII- FEMINAZI TERRORISM AND THE DICTADURE OF POLITICALLY CORRECT THOUGHT

There are three layers of imposition of this feminazi terror or dictatorship of politically correct thinking. The first, the hard core, is the feminazis that attack any dissident with the feared insult *"Male chauvinist pig"* (insult capable of ruining a person's life), in the second circle are the Demagogues (they are the ones, for opportunism of advantage policy that gives, overact their support for the feminazi flags), the third circle is the fearful (although they do not propagate in favor of the feminazis, for fear of being attacked by them, they try to hide their opinions).

An example may be the case of James Damore, an engineer with autism diagnosis, who worked at Google.

Damore's story shows the silenced injustice that occurs in reality while, in fantasy, the imaginary war against the Patriarchy occurs.

When he was a child growing up in Romeoville, a suburb of Chicago, it took longer than normal to speak in complete sentences. His parents were worried; It was several years before they discovered that their son's verbal difficulties were accompanied by extraordinary talents. At the age of 11, Damore was programming adventure games on his TI-83 calculator. He also discovered chess. In one year, he was able to compete in four chess games simultaneously while using a bandage.

Damore got a job at Google with outstanding grades and outstanding performance as a systems engineer.

One day came the Google Department of Diversity. They asked their sector about their opinions on why there were fewer female employees in Google computer jobs than male employees.

The idea that any employee can challenge the orthodoxy of the company is important in Silicon Valley, which avoids hierarchies that dominate other parts of the US. Nowhere else is this more true than Google, which cultivates open debate about thousands of internal discussion groups and online forums. Google also promotes a culture of *psychological safety* among its staff, believing that it is imperative that employees feel trained to express ideas, without feeling ashamed or judged.

Company experts say that most employees are smart enough to know that it is unwise to take that mantra "too literally." That is, everyone repeats on Google that they can express themselves and that they will be respected for their opinions, but, implicitly, it is known that there are things that are better not to say.

But when the organizers of the internal meetings on Google's policies on diversity and inclusion invited comments, Damore decided to convey his thoughts.

Damore was influenced by a well-known autism theory: Baron Cohen's hyper-masculine brain theory

Therefore, when asked why there were few women in computer science, a solitary activity where autistic people like him performed well, Damore believed he could say what he really thought and was based on different scientific papers.

His main argument was about gender.

Damore did not argue that men were better at math or coding than women, as others have. Instead, he wrote that men and women "on average" have different psychological characteristics, and this could explain why so few women choose engineering. It was based on what scientific research says: "on average", there are these genetic-based inclinations according to science. Women, Damore argued, are generally more interested in "*people than in things*" and have "*more openness directed to feelings and aesthetics.*" Both factors, he said, could explain why women prefer jobs in "social or artistic areas" rather than, for example, coding software.

Damore also applied arguments in evolutionary psychology to explain why men outperform women in positions of responsibility at Google. He cited a scientific investigation arguing that men place more importance on the physical attractiveness of a potential partner, while women value the earning capacity of a potential husband. Therefore, he wrote, men may be motivated to seek better paid jobs and women to highlight their physical beauty more.

It is important to say here that Damore did what they had asked literally: they had asked for his opinion on why he believed that there were fewer women in Google than men in computer work. But it is a very sensitive issue, a subject of many implicit codes, where it is convenient to say "*the politically correct*" and not something like what he thought.

Damore's opinion generated that the superiors criticize him. But something worse happened. His memo leaked out of Google on the internet.

Hordes of feminazis appeared demanding that Damore be fired from Google.

Of course, the problem is that his document was leaked and the feminazi hordes asked for the employee's head, that earned him his dismissal. Feminazis are a very strong pressure group because Google, the company, did not want to be exposed to being accused of a "Male chauvinist Company" which is equivalent, according to the social representations that have been imposed, to be a "Murder Company."

Therefore, in the midst of the dictatorship of politically correct thinking, Google decided to publicly criticize its dismissed employee.

Danielle Brown, Google's brand new VP of Diversity, Integrity & Governance, publicly responded to the document with a general disqualification towards Damore.

These were his words:

"Affirming our commitment to diversity and inclusion—and healthy debate

Googlers,

I'm Danielle, Google's brand new VP of Diversity, Integrity & Governance. I started just a couple of weeks ago, and I had hoped to take another week or so to get the lay of the land before introducing myself to you all. But given the heated debate we've seen over the past few days, I feel compelled to say a few words.

Many of you have read an internal document shared by someone in our engineering organization, expressing views on the natural abilities and characteristics of different genders, as well as whether one can speak freely of these things at Google. And like many of you, I found that it advanced incorrect assumptions about gender. I'm not going to link to it here as it's not a viewpoint that I or this company endorses, promotes or encourages.

Diversity and inclusion are a fundamental part of our values and the culture we continue to cultivate. We are unequivocal in our belief that diversity and inclusion are critical to our success as a company, and we'll continue to stand for that and be committed to it for the long haul. As Ari Balogh said in his internal G+ post, "Building an open, inclusive environment is core to who we are, and the right thing to do. 'Nuff said."

Google has taken a strong stand on this issue, by releasing its demographic data and creating a company wide OKR on diversity and inclusion. Strong stands elicit strong reactions. Changing a culture is hard, and it's often uncomfortable. But I firmly believe Google is doing the right thing, and that's why I took this job.

Part of building an open, inclusive environment means fostering a culture in which those with alternative views, including different political views, feel safe sharing their opinions. But that discourse needs to work alongside the principles of equal employment found in our Code of Conduct, policies, and anti-discrimination laws.

I've been in the industry for a long time, and I can tell you that I've never worked at a company that has so many platforms for employees to express themselves — TGIF, Memegen, internal G+, thousands of discussion groups. I know this conversation doesn't end with my email today. I look forward to continuing to hear your thoughts as I settle in and meet with Googlers across the company.

Thanks,

Danielle"

Google's chief executive, Sundar Pichai, told staff that Damore was dismissed because parts of his memo violated the company's code of conduct. *"Our job is to build great products for users that make a difference in their lives,"* he said. *"To suggest a group of our colleagues have traits that make them less biologically suited to that work is offensive and not OK."*

Richard Lippa of California State University, whose work the engineer cited, tells it contained a *"reasonably accurate"* summary of the research on psychological differences between men and women.

His research is similar to the "empathising-systemising theory" created by Simon Baron-Cohen, professor of developmental psychopathology at Cambridge University. He argues the female brain is predominantly hard-wired for empathy, whereas *"the male brain is predominantly hard-wired for understanding and building systems"*.

These differences, Baron-Cohen says, may explain why more men choose professions in science, technology, engineering and mathematics. Baron-Cohen also proposes people on the autism spectrum have an *"extreme male brain"*.

Cordelia Fine, a professor of psychology at the University of Melbourne, a leading feminist science writer, believes his memo made many dubious assumptions and ignored vast swaths of research that show pervasive discrimination against women. Some of Damore's ideas, she adds, are *"very familiar to me as part of my day-to-day research, and are not seen as especially controversial. So there was something quite extraordinary about someone losing their job for putting forward a view that is part of the scientific debate. And then to be so publicly shamed as well. I felt pretty sorry for him."*

The point is that what the engineer had said was not outrageous, but to suggest tendencies to explain the differences in statistics, according to very common concepts in scientific search engines.

We are not here saying that the Google employee Memo held the correct position within the scientific debate about gender, or the wrong position. But he was fired t he was fired from his office without any right to his compensation or pension

It's really not strange, because Google, in order to protect its brand image, had to take off urgently from who could be seen as "patriarchal company" and, then, had to overreact not only by publicly humiliating it from an official company statement, but also by firing it.

Damore initiated a lawsuit to Google, he is trying to make a class action with all the people who were fired from Google for their political opinions or their ideas.

A very remembered case is that of Professor Tim Hunt, British biochemist and Nobel Prize in 1993.

In 2015, he made an inappropriate joke in one of his lectures *"Let me tell you about my trouble with girls... three things happen when they are in the lab... You fall in love with them, they fall in love with you and when you criticize them, they cry. "*

His comments were tweeted by Connie St Louis, who directs the science journalism program at City University, London, and was attending the conference. She commented: *"Really, does this Nobel laureate think we are still in Victorian times?"*

Soon, this generated a hysteria of feminazis asking for Hunt's, which had become the Patriarchy symbol.

He suffered a wild campaign on social networks and then reached the written press. As a result of those words, he was branded as a "patriarchal icon". He explained that it was a joke, but it was already a scandal and nobody missed the opportunity to criticize Hunt.

He was expelled from his position as an honorary professor at the prestigious University College London.

Collegue London University, in the note that justified the decision, stated:

"UCL can confirm that Sir Tim Hunt FRS has today resigned from his position as Honorary Professor with the UCL Faculty of Life Sciences, following comments he made about women in science at the World Conference of Science Journalists on 9 June.

UCL was the first university in England to admit women students on equal terms to men, and the university believes that this outcome is compatible with our commitment to gender equality.

The title of UCL Honorary Professor is reserved for individuals who are closely linked to one of UCL's academic departments (or Institutes) and who are from a non-UCL academic/research institution. The appointee should be of an academic standing equivalent to that of Professor at UCL. It does not carry a salary, and does not ordinarily involve teaching or research at UCL, with activities undertaken in consultation with the relevant Department.

Updated statement - 15th June 2015

Sir Tim Hunt's personal decision to offer his resignation from his honorary position at UCL was a sad and unfortunate outcome of the comments he made in a speech last week. Media and online commentary played no part in UCL's decision to accept his resignation.

Sir Tim held an honorary position at UCL. He was not, and never has been, employed by UCL at any stage of his career and did not receive a salary from UCL.

UCL sought on more than one occasion to make contact with Sir Tim to discuss the situation, but his resignation was received before direct contact was established.

UCL accepted his resignation of his honorary position in good faith, and in doing so sent a clear signal that equality and diversity are truly valued at UCL. We continue to be open to engagement and dialogue on how we can best deliver on our commitment to these values."

In statements made to the BBC public network, Hunt insisted that his claims were intended to be funny, although he acknowledged that he committed "stupidity" by saying the joke of falling in love with women in the presence of students who could then reproduce the comment on social networks. But it was too late because he had installed himself as a "patriarchal macho icon" and everyone lined up to prove how politically correct they are and criticize him.

Around the world, different feminazi organizations criticized the scientist and asked that it be removed from all the places where he was.

Hunt was also detached from the Royal Society's Biological Sciences Awards Committee for that reason, and, he was also detached from the European Research Council although the scientist made efforts to explain that it was just a joke.

8 Nobel prizes were then pronounced in solidarity with Hunt, criticizing the university above all for the humiliation of expelling him, a grandiloquent and exaggerated gesture. In addition, having been expelled from all the scientific societies to which he belonged and that the same University where he was always a professor boasts of his "gender policy" seemed excessive.

Some female scientists who worked with Hunt also stressed that he was not in any way male chauvinist and that, on the contrary, he had a commitment to gender equality.

No association, no university, nobody wanted to be near Tim. The Nobel Prize and his contribution to humanity did not seem to help him.

The case of Tim Hunt also serves to exemplify and that everyone be very careful with what they say. If a Nobel Prize can be expelled from his work for upsetting these inflamed feminazis hordes, then ... What is left for an ordinary person?

Both in the cases of the Nobel Prize scientist and the fired engineer from Google, the same pattern was seen. Overreacting indignation with the sin of others is the way to promote one's holiness.

Those who go to the ceremony of burning the witch are more holy, much more holy are those who go and insult her. Google, at the time of dismissing the engineer, issued a public statement signed by the Vice President of Diversity of Google, where, while humiliating the dismissed, he could claim himself as a pluralistic company committed to pluralism.

Collegue London University, in the note that justified the decision to dismiss Hunt, presented its *"commitment to gender equality"* and also recalled that it was the first English university to accept student students, in demonstration of its commitment to equality of gender.

When a person publicly humiliates another, empathy is rarely generated towards the humiliated. When a person humiliates and discriminates against another, it rarely flaunts. Therefore, when the expulsion of the "infectious element" is done in a grandiloquent that should attract a lot of attention, something is wrong.

The Manchester Art Gallery did not content itself with eliminating the "patriarchal" artist, but also exhibited that act. It seemed to be something that served the museum authorities to show all the "gender perspective" they have.

Beyond the case of those who "make mistakes" and depart from the dictatorship of correct thinking, the vast majority, on the other hand, choose to adopt the gender ideology that has become, for an academic, a scientist, a politician, a journalist, a way of having social promotion. The reverse mechanism also occurs and is capitalized by those who wish to have a promotion.

In Tim's case, it is worth asking: If a talented Nobel Prize is expelled from a university for making a politically incorrect joke ... then how many mediocre can drive an academic career by simply repeating, as parrots, hegemonic ideas about gender?

From this perspective, the intellectual extortion suffered by men and women is enhanced by the actions of demagogues. Women who do not recognize the feminine leadership, it is because they "*lack gender awareness*", or, otherwise, because they are *"patriarchal women."* The men, for the most part, are terrified of being accused of male chauvinist.

Then the dictatorship of politically correct thinking leads to overreaction. Men, for the most part, for fear of being accused of sexists, increasingly adopt inclusive language, accept the dogmas (contrary to logic and scientific evidence) of gender ideology and thus contribute to homogenize a discourse since hold up much stronger anyone who dares to think differently.

Therefore, feminazi terror is only part of the dictatorship of correct thinking. In the second layer are the demagogues, who overreact their friendly position with the cause, to ensure that they will not be accused of "patriarchal" and, also, to shore up their own career or ascending desire for personal promotion. In the third layer are those who are afraid or cautious, avoid being targeted by the feminazi so as not to lose their jobs, submit to the imposition of *"inclusive language"* so as not to be attacked and, in some way, also contribute to homogenize speech.

In the United States the subject is in strong growth.

Recently, it was announced that the traditional feminine beauty contest "Miss America" will no longer be held with women wearing bikini. Women, instead of competing for their beauty, will highlight their intellectual achievements. The change, announced by the Board of Directors of the contest, represents an "innovative change" because the 51 applicants will no longer be judged by their physical appearance, but by "their talent and ideas."

There are several companies that also go the same way. For example, various clothing brands have begun to give in to pressure and suspend their traditional beauty pageants.

They explain that they are sensitized with "gender violence".

What does it have to do with it? Are they wars or simply beauty contests?

This, by the conspiracy theory of the Patriarchy that says a) there is an imaginary Patriarchy that silently digits the threads of society towards oppressing women b) people's behaviors are typed by the Patriarchy although they do not know c) there are murderers who kill by order of the Patriarchy, the "femicides" d) after believing all that, a brand that makes a fashion show then is a brand that works for "*The Patriarchy*" and, therefore, murders

In addition, as journalists, politicians, academics, judges, opinion makers, can improve their ladder to power only by raising these flags, what happens? The new laws and sentences continue to advance.

The issue is very delicate, because anyone who dares to criticize these hegemonic ideas of the supposed "gender violence" (is the violence attributed to the entire oppressive group), is exposed to being misrepresented, accused of being a patriarchal sexist. So, the most prudent attitude is to shut up and, meanwhile, this keeps moving forward.

On the other hand, the dictatorship of correct political thinking leads to extreme measures that every person must take to say nothing inappropriate, nothing that can be taken out of context and misrepresented. From the use of cell phones, filming, recordings, expressions in social networks, everything can be quickly viralized and public stoning of massive dimensions can be caused.

Social networks promote a society of permanent indignation that leads to any "error" of political thought becoming viral.

The television society was a society of spectators, who fed on the lives of others to fill the lack of life of their own. The society of social networks is similar, but the passive spectators of other people's lives can have a modest role:

they can look for the error of others, judge it and become indignant. Millions of people with routine lives are waiting for someone to make a mistake in order to be indignant in chorus and demonstrate their moral superiority.

Then, when some unfortunate or unfortunate person makes a wrong expression, they throw him into the bonfire of the networks and everyone does not miss the opportunity to "get indignant."

<u>**APPENDIX.**</u>

Within Feminazi authoritarianism, they have recently launched in the networks against the Royal Spanish Academy, precisely to criticize the recognition of the word "Feminazi".

Nothing less than against a linguistic authority! They want to impose on us how we should talk!

This authoritarianism, in truth, means *"how do we have to talk"* under the threat that, otherwise, we would be accused of macho and patriarchal.

But ... Why if the word feminazi is so wrong to describe these activists is so successful and growing? Why do you want to ban us from using a word?

Another form of the authoritarian operation of silence so that the word "feminazi" is not used anymore is the accusation.

The threat is: *"If you use the word feminazi, I will accuse you of trivializing or disrespecting the victims of the Holocaust"* .

It would be "trivializing" Nazism using this word. However, it is not really "trivialize it", but "humanize it". Paradoxically, considering the Nazis (as outgroup) monsters, is a Nazi attitude. Instead, humanizing Nazism is the most unpleasant, but it is the best way to prevent it. We must not seek Nazism in the other, but within us.

Especially in certain tendencies such as discrimination, simplification and hatred towards outgroups - they are immigrants, people of another skin color, people of another nationality, people of another gender, people of another sexual orientation - because it is there. It is very close. If we want to look for hate and evil, looking inside us is better.

Now, is it really a lack of respect for victims to use the word "Nazi" as an insult, to keep active the memory of what human beings are capable of doing to other human, under certain circumstances and conspiracy ideas?

Feminist authors are not so afraid of being accused of staining the victims' memories. You can think of Valerie Solanas who, in his work "Scum ", called for the extermination of all men. But, in addition, she presented the proposal to use just "Gas Chambers" as an ideal tool in her plans to exterminate those "leeches"
.

When she wrote the *"Scum Manifesto"* she already knew about the "Gas Chambers" in the Nazi Germany. So: Why does nobody talk about that being disrespectful?

From here, we recognize the importance of keeping the word "Nazi" in force - as an insult above all - to describe ideologies that follow the formula:

a- They use a characteristic of any person (such as race, gender, sexual orientation, skin color, religion, etc.) to forcefully classify them into two groups, whether or not each person is a representative of their group. You are invited to identify with the "ingroup" (group that supports the fight) and to reject the "outgroup" (group that will receive the fight).

b- The members of the outgroup are dehumanized, denying their uniqueness as people, comparing them with animals, especially animals that cause disgust - such as leeches, pigs, rats -, while the endogroup is exalted reinforcing the self-esteem of group identity .

c- A victimization of the endogroup is proposed by the outgroup, being understood as "oppressive group" and "oppressed group".

d- Conspiracy theories are used to sustain a secret and silent action through which the oppression and victimization of the oppressed endogroup is perpetuated. "Culture" is considered as the channel where the imaginary conspiracy lives.

e- The oppressor group is described as a super-powerful force so that the struggle becomes epic. The more power attributed to the oppressor group, the more pride the struggle to confront it gives. The more pride it gives, the more attractive it is. This super-powerful force would be secret, not easily visible.

The challenge is a more human way of thinking.

Each person is a sum of characteristics, it is not their race, it is not their height, it is not their skin color, it is not their gender, it is not their form of sexual desire, it is not their religious belief. Each person can deviate from the story that these "collectivist, paranoid and authoritarian ideologies" tell.

Each person is not a representative of a group, but each person is "Herself".

REFERENCIAS

Baum, W. (2005). Understanding Behaviorism: behavior, culture, and evolution (2nd ed.). Blackwell Publishing.

Becker, M., Vignoles, V. L., Owe, E., Easterbrook, M. J., Brown, R., Smith, P. B., ... & Aldhafri, S. (2014). Cultural bases for self-evaluation seeing oneself positively in different cultural contexts. Personality and Social Psychology Bulletin

Blake, K. R., Bastian, B., Denson, T. F., Grosjean, P., & Brooks, R. C. (2018). Income inequality not gender inequality positively covaries with female sexualization on social media. Proceedings of the National Academy of Sciences, 201717959.

Bordeau, J. (2009). Xenophobia: The violence of fear and hate. The Rosen Publishing Group.

Card, N. A., Stucky, B. D., Sawalani, G. M., & Little, T. D. (2008). Direct and indirect aggression during childhood and adolescence: A meta-analytic review of gender differences, intercorrelations, and relations to maladjustment. Child development, 79(5), 1185-1229.

Carley, M. J. (2016). Unemployed on the Autism Spectrum: How to Cope Productively with the Effects of Unemployment and Jobhunt with Confidence. Jessica Kingsley Publishers.

Crispin, J. (2017). Why I am not a feminist: A feminist manifesto. Melville House.

De Beauvoir, S., & Parshley, H. M. (1953). The second sex.

Deleuze, G. (2006). Post-scriptum sobre las sociedades de control. Polis. Revista Latinoamericana, (13).

Dijkstra, S. (1980). Simone de Beauvoir and Betty Friedan: The politics of omission. Feminist Studies, 6(2), 290.

Dixon, L., Archer, J., & Graham-Kevan, N. (2012). Perpetrator programmes for partner violence: Are they based on ideology or evidence?. Legal and Criminological Psychology, 17(2), 196-215

Dworkin, A. (1981). Men possessing women. New York: Perigee.

Dworkin, A. (1974). Woman hating. New York: Dutton.

Fahs, B. (2008). The radical possibilities of Valerie Solanas. Feminist Studies, 34(3), 591-617.

Feingold, A. (1990). Gender differences in effects of physical attractiveness on romantic attraction: A comparison across five research paradigms. Journal of Personality and Social Psychology, 59(5), 981.

Foucault, M. (1990). Vigilar y castigar: nacimiento de la prisión. Siglo xxi.

Foucault, M., & Lynch, E. (1980). La verdad y las formas jurídicas (Vol. 1080). Barcelona: Gedisa.

Foucault, M. (2015). Historia de la locura en la época clásica, I. Fondo de cultura económica.

Frederick, D. A., Fessler, D. M., & Haselton, M. G. (2005). Do representations of male muscularity differ in men's and women's magazines?. Body Image, 2(1), 81-86.

Fisher, H. (1994). Anatomía del amor. Barcelona: Anagrama.

Fisher, H. (2004). Why we love: The nature and chemistry of romantic love. Macmillan.

Friedan, B. (2010). The feminine mystique. WW Norton & Company.

Friedan, B. (1998). It changed my life: Writings on the women's movement. Harvard University Press.

García, A. H. P. (1994). El feminismo radical de los setenta: Kate Millet. In Historia de la teoría feminista (pp. 139-150).

Gangestad, S. W., Garver-Apgar, C. E., Simpson, J. A., & Cousins, A. J. (2007). Changes in women's mate preferences across the ovulatory cycle. Journal of personality and social psychology, 92(1), 151

Gao, W., & Smyth, R. (2010). Health human capital, height and wages in China. The Journal of Development Studies, 46(3), 466-484.

Hamermesh, D. S. (2011). Beauty pays: Why attractive people are more successful. Princeton University Press.

Haslam, N. (2006). Dehumanization: An integrative review. Personality and social psychology review, 10(3), 252-264.

Hegel, G. W. F. (2017). Fenomenología del espíritu. Fondo de cultura económica.

Hegel, G. W. F. (1970). Filosofía de la Historia. Zeus.

Hübler, O. (2009). The nonlinear link between height and wages in Germany, 1985–2004. Economics & Human Biology, 7(2), 191-199.

Jardine, A., & de Beauvoir, S. (1979). Interview with Simone de Beauvoir. Signs: Journal of Women in Culture and Society, 5(2), 224-236.

Kant, I. (2009). Crítica de la razón pura. Ediciones Colihue SRL.

Kenrick, D. T., Sadalla, E. K., Groth, G., & Trost, M. R. (1990). Evolution, traits, and the stages of human courtship: Qualifying the parental investment model. Journal of personality, 58(1), 97-116.

Márquez, N., & Laje, A. (2016). El libro negro de la nueva izquierda. Ideología de género o subversión cultural.

Laje, Agustín. (2017). El Patriarchyno existe.

Li, N. P., & Kenrick, D. T. (2006). Sex similarities and differences in preferences for short-term mates: What, whether, and why. Journal of personality and social psychology, 90(3), 468.

Lindner, K. (2004). Images of women in general interest and fashion magazine advertisements from 1955 to 2002. Sex roles, 51(7-8), 409-421.

Lopez, Tamara (2015). Hitler. Biografia Psicológica. Ediciones Historia y Presente.

Lopez, Tamara (2018). Goebbels. Biografía Psicológica. Ediciones Historia y Presente.

Millet, K. (1984). El amor ha sido el opio de las mujeres. Entrevista). El País.

Millet, K. (1990). Sexual politics; the classic analysis of the interplay between men, women and culture. New York: Simon.

Millet, K. (2000). Theory of sexual politics. Radical Feminism. A documentary reader, 122-153.

Morgan, R. (1983). The Anatomy of Freedom Feminism, Physics and Global Politics.

Morgan, R. (1980). Theory and practice: Pornography and rape. Take back the night: Women on pornography, 134-140.

Mościcki, E. K. (1994). Gender differences in completed and attempted suicides. Annals of epidemiology, 4(2), 152-158.

Nussbaum, M. (2006). El ocultamiento de lo humano. Repugnancia, vergüenza y ley. Buenos Aires. Katz

Nussbaum, M. (2014). Emociones políticas. ¿Por qué el amor es importante para la justicia? Barcelona. Paidós.

Pastor, J. (2009). Relevancia de Foucault para la Psicología. Psicothema, 21(4), 628-632.

Reilly, D., Neumann, D. L., & Andrews, G. (2015). Sex differences in mathematics and science achievement: A meta-analysis of National Assessment of Educational Progress assessments. Journal of Educational Psychology, 107(3), 645.

Rosenbaum, R. (1999). Explicar a Hitler: Los orígenes de su maldad. Siglo XXI.

Ross, M. (2018). La teoría de las hazañas escudo: una hipótesis diferente sobre la psicosis y el contenido de los delirios. Teoría y Crítica de la Psicología, (10), 25-46.

Ross, M. (2015). El M.A.S. Y EL M.A.P.: una teoría psicológica.

Rudman, L. A., & Fairchild, K. (2007). The F word: Is feminism incompatible with beauty and romance?. Psychology of Women Quarterly, 31(2), 125-136.

Ruffle, B. J., & Shtudiner, Z. E. (2014). Are good-looking people more employable?. Management Science, 61(8), 1760-1776.

Schrijvers, D. L., Bollen, J., & Sabbe, B. G. (2012). The gender paradox in suicidal behavior and its impact on the suicidal process. Journal of affective disorders, 138(1-2), 19-26.

Seibert, S. E., & Kraimer, M. L. (2001). The five-factor model of personality and career success. Journal of vocational behavior, 58(1), 1-21.

Serrano Castro, Francisco. (2012). La dictadura del género.

Solanas, V. (1968). SCUM, Society for Cutting Up Men, Manifesto. Olympia Press.

Sundie, J. M., Kenrick, D. T., Griskevicius, V., Tybur, J. M., Vohs, K. D., & Beal, D. J. (2011). Peacocks, Porsches, and Thorstein Veblen:

Conspicuous consumption as a sexual signaling system. Journal of personality and social psychology, 100(4), 664.

Tajfel, H. (Ed.). (2010). Social identity and intergroup relations. Cambridge University Press.

Van Os, J., Linscott, R. J., Myin-Germeys, I., Delespaul, P., & Krabbendam, L. (2009). A systematic review and meta-analysis of the psychosis continuum: evidence for a psychosis proneness–persistence–impairment model of psychotic disorder. Psychological medicine, 39(2), 179-195.

Vilar, E. (1973). El varón domado. Grijalbo.

Zapatero, M. D. C., & Soloaga, P. D. (2008). La representación del cuerpo de la mujer en la publicidad de revistas femeninas. Estudios sobre el mensaje periodístico, 14, 309-327.

www.ingramcontent.com/pod-product-compliance
Lightning Source LLC
Chambersburg PA
CBHW031236250726
48655CB00005B/1976